Call of the Bell Bird

Walk cheerfully over the world, answering that of God in every one

George Fox

Westminster Monthly Meeting of the Religious Society of Friends
Clerk: John Marshall, 31 Convent Gardens, Ealing, London W5 4UT
020 8568 0657, jf_marshall@yahoo.com

2 March 2001

Dear Friends

At our meeting on 18th February we recorded the following minute:

"01/33   Jennifer Kavanagh and Stephen Petter
We have learned that Jennifer Kavanagh and Stephen Petter are to travel to
North, Central and South America and to Asia and India. We send them with
our love and we send our loving greetings to those Friends whom they will meet
and we commend Jennifer and Stephen to their care."

Your loving Friend

John Marshall

[handwritten Spanish] Iglesia nacional los amigos de Arequipa.
Carmelo Ticona

[signature]   (CAROICO) 29/5/01

*20-June-01 It is a pleasure to have Jennifer Kavanagh and Stephen Petter
with us here in Monteverde. We're happy they included us in their travels.
We would like, also, to send greetings from our Meeting to yours. Interrsisit-
ation among Friends is a great aid in understanding our diversity.
In peace,
Monteverde Friends Meeting
Lucille Sheridan, clerk*

*24 June 01 Stephen & Jennifer's presence in this Sunday's meeting served as a catalyst
for worship and fellowship that was enormously rich - a true blessing.
May their ongoing journey be as graced with the Spirit as were the moments
they shared with us.   Friends Meeting   Greg Fan
Sun José Costa Rica*

2 August 01 These Friends speak our mind. Pam Daigle Arnold, clerk

Meetings at Brentford & Isleworth, Ealing, Hammersmith, Harrow, Southall, Staines & Egham, Uxbridge,
Wembley and Westminster

*Baton Rouge Friends Meeting
Baton Rouge Louisiana USA*

*Our Travelling Minute from Westminster Monthly Meeting, with the first page
of endorsements from meetings we visited*

Call of the Bell Bird

A Quaker Travels the World

by Jennifer Kavanagh

For Jocelyn
in Friendship,
Jennifer
October 2008

Quaker Books

First published November 2004 by Quaker Books

© Jennifer Kavanagh, 2004

ISBN 0 85245 365 5

Designed and typset at the Golden Cockerel Press

For Stephen, fellow traveller
and for Juliet and Guy, who held the fort

Acknowledgements

The author would like to thank all the people whose lives enriched this journey. She has made every attempt to check with them the accuracy of what she has written, and apologises for any errors that remain.

Travelling Minute reproduced by courtesy of Westminster Monthly Meeting of the Religious Society of Friends

All photographs are by the author

Contents

Prologue The Desert   9

1 Preparations   14

2 Sol y Luna   23

3 The Peacemakers   41

4 Doing the Splits   51

5 Travelling Hopefully   68

6 Home from Home   83

7 The 9/11 Factor   88

8 The Simple Life   95

9 Among Friends   104

10 Silence in Bangkok   110

11 Converging Paths   125

12 Service as Worship   143

Interlude No Man's Land   160

13 The Last Pristine Land   164

14 Resistance and Renewal   177

15 Spring   189

Epilogue   201

Further reading   202

Further information   205

The Desert

To see a World in a Grain of Sand
And a Heaven in a Wild Flower
Hold Infinity in the palm of your hand
And Eternity in an hour.

William Blake

5 a.m. October 2000. Dawn in the Western Desert, Egypt. Out of my damp blankets, fully clothed, shivering with sleepiness and the cold of the desert air to join an already sprightly Stephen. We scrambled up the long slope of sand to look down on a beautiful empty landscape: untouched dunes, small rocky hills – a vast expanse of pristine golden sand. Distant mountains like isolated islands in a sea of sand and stone and mist. We watched the sun come up, with the moon still high in the sky. We could turn and look at each, in opposite directions, with nothing in the way.

———

Ours is a stormy relationship. We had known each other for just five years at this point, and had just come together after a year of separation. During this time apart, we had each been planning a period of travel and contemplation: Stephen in Indian ashrams – he sought specifically religious surroundings – I somewhere in the desert. When Stephen read in the newspaper of monasteries in the Egyptian desert that received visitors, we agreed that this could be a perfect compromise, and a chance to prepare spiritually for the longer journey that we proposed for the following year. Our research seemed to indicate that women were accepted, but we weren't sure if we would be able to stay together or if staying at all was possible for any length of time. I was still at work so it was agreed that Stephen should go on ahead and sort things out.

When I arrived in Cairo Stephen admitted defeat. He had been sent from pillar to post in his search for the right place, until he decided to go and look for himself. The "desert" was dirty scrub with the foundations of new buildings; the monastery staff unwelcoming.

We decided to head for one of the oases on the edge of the Western Desert and bought bus tickets for Bahariya. And then, by synchronicity, Abdul, the manager of our hotel, heard of our intention to go to the desert and said he knew of just the place. It was just outside Bahariya: a safari camp that in his photos looked just perfect.

And so we came by bus, with blasting video, to the edge of the desert, several hundred kilometres from Cairo. We brought with us a few books: Aldous Huxley's *The Perennial Philosophy*, *The Desert Fathers* by Helen Waddell, *Buddhist Scriptures* and T.S. Eliot's *The Four Quartets*. We wanted to be quiet, and it was just the place. Staying in a little round brick-built hut, we walked out each day before dawn beyond the scrub into the desert, sat out of sight of each other, did yoga, read and meditated, contemplated the far horizon. When the sun got too hot we came back for breakfast, did some practical chores, had a rest and returned to the desert about 4 p.m., reading, leaning up against a eucalyptus or palm, until sundown. As darkness descended, we lay on the sand behind shrubs, near, but out of sight of, the road. We watched the stars come out and listened to the clip clop of donkeys and carts laden with large bundles of hay and other animal foodstuffs, carrying farmers back from their labours, some of them singing as they went.

But I wanted more. Having come all this way, I wanted to be in the desert, away from people, the two of us alone. As we researched the possibilities, I was eager, Stephen wary but in agreement. I could see me finding it hard to come back again. I had such a longing for that isolation, sleeping under the stars – it was what I had come for.

We managed to persuade our new friend Yahyah and his colleagues at the hotel to drive us out deep into the desert and leave us there, picking us up four days later. They would give us a tent for protection against the sun, blankets (they had no sleeping bags) and a supply of water. We went out to buy food in the small oasis town: dates, bananas and tomatoes, flat brown bread, cheese, olives and a tin of beans. Enough for four days.

Where they left us was not as featureless as I would have liked, but beautiful all the same, at the edge of massive sand dunes, under a line of black granite hills. Alone, with no sound or sight of another human being. Wonderful.

We soon found that the tent was useless. The camp staff's experience was limited to organising large parties to spend one night in the desert with a big army tent for protection. Yahyah had borrowed his wife's plastic bell tent, in which we would have fried. We put some of our stores in it and weighed it down with rocks against the power of the wind. Stephen, who thankfully has the practical gene, had brought string, and rigged up a shelter with our blankets and a stick at each corner, under which we could crawl during the powerful heat of the middle hours. The matches they had given us only lasted for one brew up, so we had no means of heating water, or ourselves at night.

I wept when we first arrived – at last, stretching into the far horizon, was the golden sand of my dreams, the immeasurable space. We decided on one spot for sleeping, one for washing and eating, and another, up the hill, for lavatorial activities. Such emptiness; such

Our encampment: sheltering from the sun.

freedom. We soon found a routine: crawling out of bed just before dawn to greet the sun at the top of the nearby sand dune. Breakfast, a long walk, then sitting in the shelter of a rock to read, exercise, meditate, again out of sight of each other, but within earshot, just in case. We came back for lunch, then crawled back under our blanket shelter, to sleep, and read T.S. Eliot – extraordinarily apt – to each other. Cowering away from the sun, grateful for the wind; long hours waiting for the day to cool down. We held Meetings for Worship, just the two of us, morning and evening. They were not always successful, but sometimes by reading from our little book of Quaker Advices and Queries, or by recollecting the members of our Meeting, we would feel them with us, and enter into a deeper silence. I had taken off my watch, content to tell the time from the sun and my hunger pangs; Stephen I knew cheated, and looked at his from time to time.

After sunset the temperature dropped. Neither of us slept well – we were cold and restless on the hard ground. But once fully clothed, with a scarf round my head to protect it from the wind, I was reasonably comfortable. On the first night the stars covered the sky with pinpricks of light; a coverlet of diamonds. After that the full moon took over and lit up the whole area. On my night-time visits to the loo patch, my path was clear before me, and I stood and looked around me, at first nervous, then revelling in the white-lit emptiness.

During the day, for the first time since babyhood, I walked naked – for once shedding the self-consciousness of ordinary life, taking with me only a T-shirt against the strength of the sun. Stephen was amused, and admiring of my courage – but what was there to be courageous about? We were the only people there.

We treasured what little signs of life we saw: a solitary shoot of grass or other plant, bravely pushing out of the sand; a hovering bird of prey, even some swallows; though we were less keen on the occasional fly that got blown along to us from more populous places. We were intrigued by a very beautiful track in the sand, a lace-like tracery. To our surprise it turned out to be the track of a large black beetle that I had found in my shoe the previous day. Its footprints were so pretty, so delicate, quite unlike the beast itself, but it gave us great pleasure to watch it plodding along the sand leaving its artistic trail.

And the desert fox appeared around supper time. It was obviously not frightened of us, and only in search of food, but, despite my best intentions, I was scared. He was silver, skinny, a wraith slinking about in the moonlight, and he gave me the shivers. Stephen gave him water and later half-heartedly threw stones to chase him away, but he reappeared every night.

I read of the wisdom of the Desert Fathers, who had lived in this same desert for many years, seeking spiritual development and slow growth. I read too the Buddha's eight-fold path:

Right belief
Right will
Right speech
Right action
Right means of livelihood
Right effort towards self-control
Right attention or collectedness
Right contemplation

The Perennial Philosophy, a classic work on the universality of the mystic core of religion, was an invaluable part of our little library. In it St Catherine of Siena is quoted: To know God without self-knowledge leads to presumption; to know self without God leads to despair.

The desert, our solitude and our reading had a profound effect on both of us. Although bad nights made us tetchy, we did achieve moments of great physical, emotional and spiritual closeness. We felt blessed in being able to share such an experience, and felt our spiritual preparation in Egypt boded well for our larger journey the following year.

CHAPTER I

Preparations

For every day will be Sunday to thee, and wherever thou goest thou wilt have a
priest, a church, and an altar along with thee.

William Law

When Stephen and I told friends of our plan to backpack round
the world for a year, responses were mostly envious – "Can you
take me in your suitcase?" Some people asked where we were going; a
few asked, "What for?" I was 54, Stephen ten years older; perhaps this
was not predictable behaviour.

I was born of a family that travelled – though not always from
choice. My mother is Russian, but had to leave St Petersburg at the age
of five. Her family then moved on to Latvia and finally Switzerland,
where she was brought up. Her first marriage took her to Egypt for
ten years, where she met my father who brought her to England. My
father was brought up in Peru and, in his work for the Colonial Office,
spent a great deal of time in Africa. When I was five we spent a year in
Malaya. Travel was in the blood: it was no wonder that I had itchy feet.
But bringing up my two children, then plunging into my own business,
meant that my desire to travel had to go underground for a while. Once
my children were independent, the possibility became a reality.

The birth of this particular journey lay in a heartfelt need to
make connection with some far-flung friends who had been significant
influences on my life, especially my spiritual life. I came to recognition
of a spiritual life quite recently. Only after my marriage broke up in
1987 did I realise an overwhelming need for another dimension. When,
after several years of seeking, I found Friends (the Religious Society of
Friends, known as Quakers) my life changed.

Their practice of silent unmediated worship–no priests, or
rather "the priesthood of all believers" – spoke to me. They have no

creed – faith is dynamic; what we believe today may not be the same as that which we believe tomorrow. A faith that is lived through testimonies to peace, truth, equality and simplicity. I found a community of independent spirits, taking responsibility for their lives and for the betterment of the world. From a lifetime of feeling that I couldn't make a difference to poverty and injustice, I found myself among people who were making a difference; in small ways, individuals were quietly showing by example that life could be better.

For some years after that transition, I assumed that my finding of Friends had come out of the blue – no Quakers in my family – then realised that I had had unrecognised signposts all along the way. In a period of a few months, a series of encounters with people from my past made me realise that Quakers had always been there in my life: I had simply not been ready to embrace them.

So it was as a consolidation of that recognition that I wanted to pursue other friendships that I knew had spiritual significance for me, friendships that might help to answer the question "Who is there that can tell me who I am?" There was Samuel in a remote village in Kenya, a young Roman Catholic priest with whom I have been corresponding since meeting at Taizé, the ecumenical monastery in France that I had visited in the years of my seeking. There was Lucinda. Like me, a former literary agent, she had given up work a few years before me, and is now running retreats both in Italy and in her home town of Toronto, Canada. There was Sasha, outside Moscow. We had also met at Taizé, and he had come over to stay with us one Christmas and told us of how tough life was in Russia.

Martha also came from my life as an agent. A writer and translator from the Chinese, she had fallen in love with Mongolia and now lives there for part of the year. She had set up a weaving cooperative with her own money and was something of a role model for me. And there was my cousin in Guatemala to whom I had always been close; a publishing friend in Sydney whom I hadn't seen for years; and a member of our Quaker Meeting who had sold up and emigrated, and was currently travelling round Australia.

A second strand of motivation was born out of a discomfort with my own affluent lifestyle. In the world of publishing for nearly thirty years, I had begun to feel increasingly out of synch with the prevailing mores. It was a comfortable world, and an insular one. I felt there were other worlds to explore and other work to be done: it was a dissatisfaction not only with my work but with my place in a "glamorous" arena – a glamour I had never believed in. When I became a Quaker, I found the impetus to move on, to move outwards and involve myself in the wider world. I sold my literary agency and worked, first of all as a volunteer, then as an employee for a Quaker charity in the East End of London, in the fifth most deprived ward in England. I was asked to start a community centre in this largely Bangladeshi area, from which stemmed an initiative to help the mostly refugee and immigrant local women to found their own businesses. Our microcredit programme was born.

I had also been working with homeless people in central London, people whose lives had slipped out of gear. They were often divorced men who had left their houses to their wives and children, feeling they could manage, then slipping into drink as life overcame them; young people leaving "care" or abusive homes; men leaving prison or the army, unable to cope after the protection of institutional life. After those four years working with men and women who live in this country in poverty and deprivation, I wanted to spend time in developing countries, experience for myself how most people in the world live. I had moved outwards from one world to a very different one. It had given me a hunger to see more.

Then, as my partner Stephen and I came back together, we began to discuss the idea of travelling, and other ideas came up. Stephen had lived in Florida and Hawaii and wanted to revisit them. If we were to go to the States, I could visit friends in Florida and I'd always wanted to see the desert in the south-west. Stephen had relations in San Francisco and also in British Columbia to which he had been evacuated in the war. We had both always wanted to go to India, and this became the centrepiece of our trip.

In particular, Stephen had a strong motivation to travel "among Friends", to visit Quakers in other parts of the world, especially those living isolated from any local Meeting. We are a small faith worldwide, about 200,000, and generally pleased to receive visitors of like mind and heart. "Travelling in the Ministry" is a traditional form of service among Friends; we would be tiptoeing in the footsteps of many fine people. Despite the dangerous conditions, extensive travel to other Meetings was commonplace in the seventeenth and eighteenth centuries. In the early days of Quakerism, the Valiant Sixty travelled all over England, proclaiming their faith; some went to Holland, even to Russia. John Woolman came from the States to England, arriving late for the Yearly Meeting of Quakers there because he refused to use stage-coaches which he felt mistreated the horses. Susanna Morris from Philadelphia, who died in 1755, travelled back and forwards across the Atlantic, the last time at the age of 70, despite having endured three shipwrecks on her previous voyages. Nothing that we could do could begin to come up to the valour of these stalwart Quaker souls.

Nonetheless, the blessing of our Meeting was important to us and we asked for and were given a "travelling minute" – a letter from our Meeting to take with us as an introduction, to be endorsed by each Meeting that we visited. To our surprise, before we left we were asked to address a gathering of some thirty Friends about our plans for the journey. The warmth of our send-off was unexpected, and one Friend thrust a fiver into my hand to give to any worthwhile project we might come across. Stephen and I had been so absorbed in the practicalities of our preparations that we hadn't had time to realise the emotional power of such a leave-taking. It is hard to explain how important the support of our Meeting was throughout our journey; we felt it with us everywhere we went. Each time our minute was endorsed, each time we received an email from a member of our Meeting, we felt the warmth of its embrace.

Our original idea was simply to go, and let ourselves be guided by the Spirit about when to move on and where. This would have enabled us to involve ourselves fully in a project if it presented itself, without constraint. In the event the only affordable method was to buy a round the world ticket which demanded a route and a (changeable) timetable. In the planning, our newly re-established relationship trembled under the tensions of our differing points of view (I really didn't want to spend so much time in first-world countries; Stephen didn't want to go to South America or Mongolia) but compromises were eventually made. We were both concerned that we were not going to be staying anywhere long enough to make a difference, that we would always be "passing through", but we realised that we would have to consider it as a series of "tasters"; perhaps we would find a place or a project to which we wanted to return.

Planning the trip was time-consuming. Fortunately, my son Guy works in the travel industry and was able to sort out a route that fitted in with the demands of the ticket: up to 15 stops, 39,000 miles, and one year. Though we did not want to be tied down, it was important for us to contact the people we wanted to see – and this included Quakers on a list of isolated Friends, and Meetings in various parts of the world. Despite my Luddite tendencies, I learned how to communicate on email, and contacted dozens of people all over the world. I tried to alternate "easy" and "difficult" countries – I knew some places would be tougher than others, and in many places we had no contacts.

I was determined to go somewhere for a holiday before launching into the journey proper. Brazil had not been on our original list, but when my son suggested a place on the Brazilian coast I remembered bumping into a publishing friend who had mentioned that she had bought a house there. Feeling very cheeky, I phoned her and she and her partner very kindly allowed us to use it.

So, the decision was made to go to:

Brazil, for a holiday;
Peru – my father was brought up there, and I wanted to see it, as well as the Mayan ruins;
Bolivia and Costa Rica for the many Quakers there;
Honduras where Stephen had been for a conference;
Guatemala, to visit my cousin;

then the States and Canada – we decided to drive through the South from Florida to L.A. and then up the West Coast into British Columbia;

Hawaii, where Stephen had lived;

Tonga. I was very keen to visit a South Sea island, and Stephen wanted to do some sailing, so after a lot of juggling Guy managed to get us to Tonga;

then to New Zealand and Australia – Friends in both countries encouraged us to extend our planned few days there;

Thailand, originally mainly because it was a Buddhist country, but increasingly to visit isolated Friends;

three months in India, with a commitment to volunteer at a number of projects, also to particular ashrams and a wish to see, for instance, the Himalayas;

then to Singapore to catch a plane to Beijing, again only for a few days, to catch the Trans-Siberian Express to

Mongolia, and on to Russia – Moscow to see Sasha, and St Petersburg, my mother's birthplace;

last stop, Stockholm, not on our list, but beautiful, and the home of my singing teacher!

It was simply not possible to go to Africa on our ticket. I would have to visit Samuel another time.

We were invited to stay by relations and Quakers, and we joined Servas, an organisation of international peace and friendship, members of which host travellers for a couple of nights – a magnificent way of meeting local like-minded people.

The timing of the trip was crucial. Stephen, having come to the end of his computer programming contract a couple of years short of retirement age, was free to leave his freelance work; two of the projects I had been working on had come to fruition, so I too was able to leave. After lifetimes of bringing up children and working we were free. I rejected any notion of "a year out". For Stephen it was a year of transition to a new life; for me it was the next step in a journey that had started with my leaving the world of publishing. For both of us, the journey was a spiritual one. Quakerism is not a cut and dried religion: it is a way of life and a community of seekers. This trip was an expression of our way of life and a context for our seeking. As a form of outreach, we had printed visiting cards with our names and "Quaker Travellers" on them. If people were interested, they would ask, and it would provide an opening for conversation.

The practicalities of going away for a year were formidable. Financially we were able to go because we each had some savings to pay the fare, and our weekly budget for the year was established by the rent we received for our flats in London – perfectly adequate for living in third-world countries; tight in, for instance, the USA. But we wanted to travel simply, on local buses and trains, eating local food and staying in the homes of local people or in backpackers' hostels. I knew from experience that travellers cheques were no use in some countries, so we decided mainly to rely on ATMs abroad, though I did take some dollar travellers cheques for emergencies, together with some currency for our first stop.

We bought rucksacks – wonderful new versions that had optional wheels. For wrinklies like us it was essential not always to have to carry our stuff, and in the event we used the wheels most of the time. Water bottles, torches, sheet sleeping bags (Guy had bought me a luxurious plum-coloured silk one to pamper me on the trip), mosquito net, heavy duty insect repellent (DEET) for the jungle. We had a battery of jabs, but decided against those for rabies and Japanese encephalitis. We were given conflicting advice about the use of malarial prophylactics: increasingly the view is that it affects indigenous people badly if the drugs used by them as medicine for malaria are also used by visitors as deterrent. But in the end we bowed to our doctor's advice.

We were anxious to travel light, and took a minimum of clothes – for hot weather only, as the cold countries came at the end of our trip, and we decided that we could buy padded clothes in Beijing. Nonetheless, we both ended up with an extra bag. My weakness was for books: not only a guide book for each of the first countries, but dictionaries/phrase books and books to read that were relevant to that country: Marquez and *The Power and the Glory* for Latin America, Faulkner and Steinbeck for the States, the Upanishads and other Hindu scriptures for India and Tolstoy for Russia. I also carried a portable CD player with a dozen or so favourite CDs. Stephen took a short-wave radio and a number of practical items, such as compass, string, pliers, emergency blanket (a piece of foil), blow-up cushion etc. I decided to send some things ahead to the States and to Australia, where friends kindly agreed to receive them – mainly books, but also modest clothes specifically for India. I had been to Bangladesh a few years earlier and had bought a couple of *salwar kameezes* at Whitechapel market for the purpose. Practical loose trousers and tunic, with scarf draped to hide any notion of female form, they make life easier, and are a courtesy to local sensibilities.

A large portion of my extra bag was taken up with dozens of bottles of pills. In January, three months before we were due to depart, I was assailed by violent night sweats, hot flushes and mood swings. Belatedly, the menopause was upon me, and my energy was depleted, just as I needed it most. I was adamant about not taking HRT so I went to a Chinese herbalist. It was evident that I could not take a vast volume of herbs with me, or indeed brew them up en route, so the doctor gave me phials of little black pills, a whole phial to be swallowed morning and night. Enough for three months, the little bottles rattled as we went.

A lot of the work was in planning for our absence rather than for our trip. My daughter kindly agreed to check our mail; I gave my son power of attorney to deal with any problems that came up. My mother agreed to store my belongings, and Stephen's sister stored his. The flat was to be let furnished but we had to remove personal possessions: thousands of books, records, clothes, pictures etc. My children borrowed a number of pictures, books and discs, all of us knowing that they would find it hard to return some of them! I gave post-dated cheques to my accountant for the income tax; I put everything on direct debit, including my credit card. To let the flat, I had to buy a lot of new equipment – the tatty things we were quite happy with would not be appropriate for anyone else. The bed that had been propped up with books for years had to go, as did the oven with a wonky door. Both items that could be mended easily in countries such as Egypt or India, but no one would do it here.

I had always avoided learning Spanish. I speak French and Italian and didn't want to confuse myself but, faced with three months in Latin America, I knew that the time had come. Stephen, who does not find languages easy, went to Spanish classes for some time before we left. We had originally planned to leave in early March, so I had left work a month earlier to give me time to get ready. Stephen was unhappy at the idea of missing his last meeting of the Quaker European committee he was on so, in the end, we deferred our trip until mid-April. This meant I had a lot of time to prepare, not only in practical terms, but mentally. Whereas Stephen was working until the last moment, I had been thinking of the year ahead for some time.

Our flight was to leave at 2200 hours on April 18th, 2001. At two o'clock that morning Stephen turned to me and said, "I think we should put this off for a bit; I don't feel ready to go." I then spent most of the day accompanying my daughter to court where she was appearing as a witness – our usual lives and responsibilities were still pulling at us, and I found parting from my children unutterably hard.

But at last, after all those hours, days, years, we were free, ready to go. Armed with passports, spare photos for the visas that would have to be obtained later on in the trip, a book full of airline tickets and a filofax full of addresses, we set off for Heathrow, and a 13-hour trip to our first stop, Rio.

On the eve of our journey I wrote in my journal:

People ask "Where are you going?" then one or two ask "What for?" A good question and hard to answer. To gain a new perspective, from seeing how life is in developing countries, away from the spoilt affluence of this insular part of the world; to learn to be less busy, to respond to the Spirit, to be more spontaneous; to be useful, humble, learning and contributing, to try to live in the present and respond to the needs that present themselves. It will change us – who knows how?

Sol y Luna

*You never enjoy the world aright till the Sea itself floweth in your veins, till
you are clothed with the heavens, and crowned with the stars: and perceive
yourself to be the sole heir of the entire world, and more than so, because men
are in it who are every one sole heirs as well as you.*

Thomas Traherne, *Centuries of Meditations*, 1:27–31

We began with a holiday.

Stephen and I started as we continued: at odds. I found our two
weeks in Brazil an idyll; Stephen was bitten to bits, made it clear he did
not want to be there, and spent most of his time listening to the BBC
World Service and brushing up his Spanish – we were in a Portuguese-
speaking country. He had not had time to prepare mentally, and had
not adjusted to the travelling mode. We each thought we might have
been better travelling alone.

The first morning we awoke to the most glorious view I had
ever seen from a bedroom window. Dawn over the bay, mist, islands,
an amazing variety of bird calls – I wished I knew more about birds.
I watched a fisherman near our shore. The banging we had heard in
the night obviously came from someone like him banging the side
of his boat to frighten the fish into the net. The butterflies were large,
numerous and brilliantly coloured: a big primary yellow one hanging
from a bush like a sere leaf; a bright orange one flitting through the
trees; a mottled green one blending in with the background. Sometimes
it was difficult to tell the difference between them and the tiny birds.

I spent most of my time on the little beach just over the crest of
the hill from Casa Azul where we were staying, past a neighbour's house.
The first morning, tide out, it looked completely idyllic: clean and empty,
just the hum of voices to remind me of a little habitation at the back of
the beach, and the odd cock crow. I swam very quietly and slowly the
length of the shore, gazing at the palms and the rich variety in size and

colour of other foliage, with an occasional look out to the islands in the bay. There was a vulture on the tallest jack fruit palm, no sound but the ripples of the sea, a cicada, the occasional bird. As I dozed in the shade, I felt uneasy at a rustling behind the rocks at the back of me. Two guinea fowl and an unidentified bird halfway to a turkey jumped down. A hen appeared ten yards from me; a miniature farmyard on the beach.

It was the greatest tranquillity I had known for a long while. The air was balmy – autumnal by local standards; it was midday and we were near the equator. As I sat on my sarong, reading, I watched the tide come in, reaching nearer to where I sat, like a welcomed familiar visitor, calm, insistent, very much at my level. Behind me a breeze loosened crackling leaves on to the path. The cockles on the boulder in front of me showed a high water mark of nearly two feet above its present level. In how many places can you lie alone for hours on a beach of such beauty, in glorious unbroken sunshine? Yellow butterfly, red butterfly, the cheep of birds, the hum of a distant boat, and the eternal sound of the sea. Paradise.

Benedita was a marvel. She was young and fit – we could not believe she was forty – married with children. Unfailingly cheerful, she came over every day to clean the lovely house and cook for us, ferrying herself from the nearby island in a dug-out canoe. I found myself catapulted into unfamiliar Portuguese, discussing meals and shopping. Misunderstandings arose: when Benedita asked if we would like a *bola*, I, thinking she had said *pollo* (chicken), started to discuss dinner, then found that she was actually asking if we would like cake for breakfast. My efforts brought back the intense pleasures of language, even at the basic level, and interactions between different tongues. How can *cerveza* be so different from beer, *birra, bier, bière?* How can the words for thank you be so varied – *gracias* and *grazie*, but then *merci, danke* and thanks and most of all the Portuguese *obrigado* which agrees with the gender of the speaker ("obliged"). I remember saying to a friend that if I took up study again it would be of either theology or comparative linguistics. He said that the subjects were not so different: seeking the unity in language was spiritual too.

The humidity that kicked in every evening was hard to cope with, as were the attendant insects and the lack of electricity. There was a little light powered by solar energy but not enough to read by. Music, conversation or sleep – a seductive choice as we struggled with jet lag – were our only options indoors, whereas the magical night of the outdoors, with fireflies dancing in the trees, satellites coursing across the sky and lights across the water, was fraught with the attack of the insects. In general we ate our fine fish dinners and vast salads outside, plastered in insect repellent.

We had a glorious day exploring some of the hundreds of islands in the bay, Stephen sunny again, his hand in mine. A pretty little boat with an engine, a blue cover and a charming *marinheiro*, Paulo. Islands with beautiful beaches, where we luxuriated in the limpid water, islands with shoals of brightly coloured fish that practically leapt into our hands. I had to pinch myself sometimes to remind myself where I was. Flying is such a sudden medium of travel. Such vivid fish gave me a more realistic sense of the exotic place we were in. Words like "exotic", "tropical", "jungle", seemed to have an existence apart from the actuality of being there, and seemed external, larger than life, like the artificial notion of glamour.

But I was aware that this was time out; that we had not yet started our journey proper. This was luxurious living, quite separate from the life of the local fishing community. We had caught glimpses of the poverty around us – on the beach, I glimpsed a painfully thin old woman flitting through the trees in a straw hat and cotton frock. On a trip over to Benedita's island, we walked through local hamlets, and felt more in touch with a local reality. Dogs, a noisy school, and snapshots that would be too intrusive to photograph – a gap-toothed old woman squatting by a water hole, washing her pots and pans, a younger woman with children sitting in a canoe inland in the shade, with her husband, back to us, mending nets behind her. And, up on the hill behind our house, we saw a poor old white horse, thin and ill, chained up to die. No one could afford the vet's bills.

Everywhere, there were vultures. Sinister, ugly, scraggy birds with ancient necks, like turkeys. Stephen said they walked sideways, evilly. Would we think them so ugly if we weren't aware of their reputation? If, say, they were like turkeys? Why should we think worse of those that eat dead flesh than those who kill to eat?

This first holiday period contained within it some of the strands that were to persist throughout the year: an uncomfortable sense of a divided world, with its co-existent wealth and poverty, and the first glimpse of how the natural world was to affect me on this journey, how the richness of animal life was to penetrate and deepen my consciousness.

There is no quiet place in the white man's cities.
No place to hear the unfurling of leaves in spring or the rustle of insects' wings.

Words by Ted Perry, based on Chief Seattl's speech to
the President of the United States in 1854

We were not at our best in cities. Before we left England I was pretty sure that when we got back I would want to move out of London. I was sick of noise and the pressure of everyday living. I certainly had no wish to spend time in South American cities which all the guide books agreed were simply springboards to the historic sights and the magnificence of the natural world of the Andes, the Amazon and the jungle.

Stephen, however, had European expectations of cities: the art galleries and museums, the central cultural experiences, and wanted to stay in Lima, La Paz, Managua or San José. In each we argued, Stephen feeling that he was not seeing what he wanted; I desperate to get out to the world that I had come for. It was a pattern that was to recur throughout our trip. My need to get out into the natural world was a powerful instinct: to unite with that of God in all creation.

In Peru, we travelled the well-worn tourist path from Lima to Nazca, to Arequipa, to Cuzco and Machu Picchu, staying mostly with Servas hosts, and staying long enough in a hotel in Arequipa to settle a little, shopping in the market and cooking for ourselves. On hearing that Stephen's birthday coincided with Mother's Day – a festival second only to Christmas in the Peruvian calendar – our former hosts in Arequipa invited us to lunch. Arriving, as asked, at 1 p.m., we were embarrassed to realise that our hosts, Jorge and Ludwig, were not ready – we were not expected to arrive on time. We finally ate after 3 p.m. In the interim we got to know the brothers better. Ludwig, unlike most of the people we met abroad, did not eulogise Margaret Thatcher but asked us what we thought of her.

"Margaret devil," he said in agreement, then added, "Diana angel." My heart sank as he took our silence for agreement, and it fell to my boots as he insisted on playing a double CD of the music played at Princess Diana's funeral.

As we journeyed from one town to the next, we had our first taste of the delights of overland travel and the grandeur of the Andes. Decorated by intricate pre-Columbian terracing, and of a scale unknown to Europeans, they towered above and below us, as we scaled them by bus, up to a level of nearly 5,000 metres, chewing coca leaves to combat the effects of altitude. The local bus itself was full of life. One member of a family had been left behind, then caught up by taxi, only to find that his mother had gone back to find him. Another

Machu Picchu

mother and daughter carefully processed up the aisle of the bus, carrying the layers of a wedding cake; vendors offered food up to the windows or came on board with biscuits, cake, luminous drinks, pens. These journeys of up to twelve hours were only spoilt by the paucity of pee breaks. We felt that Indians must have iron bladders. The stops, when they occurred, allowed only for desperation. On one occasion, we could look down from the road on the hamlet, and into the open lavatories, where women squatted beside buckets in open stalls. No doors, no roof, only the lowest of walls. I envied the Indian women their voluminous skirts.

Strangely, it was on two organised "tours" in Peru – something we avoided all year – that we had two of our richest experiences of the natural world. The first was to visit the Colca Canyon. There were certainly tiresome elements in the trip that confirmed my prejudices, such as the overcostumed line-up of local people which posed for us in one village, or a folklorique evening best passed over: locals on display to tourists rather than an interaction aiming at some common understanding. But we did manage to abscond from an overpriced communal evening meal to find a local one, where a village band happened to be practising for its own pleasure.

The canyon itself was awesome. Twice as deep as the Grand Canyon in the States, it is one of the few spots where condors can be seen close to, rising on the warm early morning thermals. There was a slight touch of photojournalistic rush at the sight, but in general a hushed constraint. Stephen and I walked ahead of the bus, each settling separately to some quiet contemplation of the scene: flowers and cacti, hummingbirds, and a red kestrel, as we picked our way back through a natural rockery of stones and plants.

Chivay, where we stayed for those couple of days, was a splendid little Indian town, full of bustle; on the tourist trail but thoroughly self-possessed. As we wandered among the stalls selling maté tea with different herbs, and dishes of chicken, maize and rice, we were struck by the richness and dignity of local life. There's an uneasy balance in the contact between people as wealthy as we are and those whose country we invade with diesel fumes and the dust thrown up by our four-wheel drives, but they need our custom, and on the whole the exchanges were friendly and dignified. The begging of some small children and the posing for cameras demeaned us all.

Chivay was the first area where I felt in the right place, somewhere where a real connection might be possible. We both gloried in the landscape and the people, wished that we could remain to walk at length and embed ourselves a little.

———

Throughout our time in Peru I was itching to get to the Amazon and the jungle. I feel a gravitational pull towards grandeur and wilderness, nature at its most elemental. We found that to get to the Amazon proper at Manaus, we would have to fly back via Lima at great expense, and Stephen did not in any case like the idea of several days' journey by boat on open deck – in his mind mosquitoes loomed large. So, feeling sore and with a bad grace, I settled for our second "tour": three days in the jungle near Puerto Maldonado on the Madre Dios, one of the tributaries of the Amazon. Sleep did not figure much at this point in our journey: the overnight buses, the early starts, 5.30 a.m. to catch our plane to Puerto Maldonado, 5.30 for our first day in the jungle and an effortful 4.30 to catch the plane back.

But in between were two days of the most profound experience. For the first time the image and the experience matched. The jungle, like the desert and the mountains, lives up to the expectation. And my courage was stretched. On a 15km hike through the jungle, my fear at walking over swamp, on a walkway just one or two planks wide with rotting handrails, was transformed after two kilometres from a tentative balancing act into upright strolling. The climb up 95 rickety steps into a tree platform to look down on to jungle that clutched my stomach in advance, and to some extent on the way up, turned on the way down into the surefootedness of my youth.

There was a strong sense of the closeness of local people to the land and its fruits. Our guide pointed out the use that local people made of every plant – for building houses, as tools, for medicinal use or to eat. We were warned not to lean on or touch the "justice tree". There is a symbiotic relationship between the tree and the lines of ants that on close inspection could be seen crawling up the bark. One sting would be extremely painful; a few would mean death. In the past, wrongdoers had been tied up to these trees, and left to die.

What impressions! The howling monkeys sounding like the wind rushing through trees before dawn, the caymans or alligators sunning themselves on the banks or submerged, just the red of their eyes visible in the torch beams from the boat at night; the Madre Dios herself, wide, viscous, fast-flowing through Bolivia into the Amazon.

There was no hot water but welcome tropical heat. No electricity except in the bar and restaurant; but candles, a lantern for each bungalow, the covered walkway lit by oil lamps. Our fears of a package were unfounded: only three other guests, nothing luxurious, little feeling of being managed or packaged. Certainly no mollycoddling.

At last came a day of connections. Life on the trip so far had felt disjointed, agreeable but without substantial meaning. Like pieces of a jigsaw with not only the rest missing but not even the possibility of a jigsaw in sight. Then something happens and all falls into place. Thus, we went one day to our first Quaker Meeting in South America, and my first evangelical one.

There are different kinds of Quakers in the world, and none knows much about the others, though each claims to be the authentic kind. When William Penn and others went out to the United States in the seventeenth century, and founded Quakerism over there, there was a compulsion, as with other radicals, to keep going West. As they went, they built new churches and were influenced by the evangelical nature of those around them. Gradually, Western American Quakerism became evangelical, programmed and pastor-led, and a great split occurred in the early nineteenth century. The evangelical branch spread to Africa and Latin America, leading to a situation in the present day of very different strands of Quakerism in different parts of the world.

We knew that in South America we were going to encounter Quakers of the programmed evangelical persuasion but, as Friends from the country in which Quakerism was born, we were keen to show solidarity. And the Friends church in Arequipa, Peru, certainly gave us a warm welcome. Almost entirely Indian, the congregation of about two hundred expressed their faith in three hours of singing, clapping and preaching. It was a million miles from our own largely silent practice, but a moving occasion as they greeted the first foreign Quakers to have visited them.

The connection came from the presence of a pair of US Quaker missionaries. It's a strange concept for contemporary liberal Friends, although there were in fact British Quaker missionaries into the mid-twentieth century. Ken and Tanya, it turned out, were only in Arequipa by chance. They actually lived with their home-schooled daughter some miles away in Puno and after 13 years were about to go back to the States. Unlike the pastors of other evangelical churches, they had groomed their successors. It was time to leave the leadership of the church in the hands of local people, and they had come to Arequipa to say goodbye. They told us that they were planning to spend a day visiting Quakers in outlying Indian pueblos, and invited us to join them. Although I am uncomfortable with the missionary intent, it was a kind offer, and we felt privileged to be asked.

Our day with them the following week was mind-expanding. We had arrived the previous night in Puno, a pretty frontier town on the shores of Lake Titicaca which, at 3,827 metres (12,500 feet), is the highest lake in the world. Ken and Tanya picked us up from our hotel at 8.30 a.m. and drove about 60km to an extraordinary Aymaran Indian community on the Alto Plano. Extraordinary because the houses were concrete rather than adobe – the original ones had been destroyed in the floods of 1985 – and because of the density of the population – apparently the most densely populated rural community in the world. Having been to Bangladesh, it was hard to believe.

Visiting an Aymaran pueblo

Reuben, a quiet, humble man, is a Quaker pastor and a former clerk of Yearly Meeting. He took us to see a building on an island in the middle of the reed bed edges of Lake Titicaca near his home, which serves as a centre for meetings in the community. We reached it by boat, punted by Reuben: a magical journey through the reeds, with coots, an ibis and other birds wheeling round us.

We went back to their concrete hut for lunch. It was cooked but not eaten by his wife Victoria who had been breastfeeding their 11-month-old daughter when we arrived. It was a huge meal mainly of root vegetables, dry and hard to eat without a drink, which is not served until afterwards. Ken then preached and prayed for some time, then all present said a little in Spanish before embracing each other in a warm farewell – the two couples had come to know each other well after 13 years.

In the car Ken described the subtle and complex interactions between Christianity and Aymaran beliefs and superstitions. He had made a ten-year study of Aymaran customs; in common with most ancient peoples, they live close to the land and retain a connection with the power of the natural world that we have lost. As we drove, Ken pointed out a mountain top which he called "the highest altar in the world". Human sacrifice to the devil is still practised there to bring financial luck, as it is in the mines to the god of the underworld. The victim is often a girl brought from elsewhere who has no idea what is happening.

At a neighbouring house we were awaited in some distress by an old man and his family. They had asked Ken to come and pray with them to stem the tide of ill luck they had experienced, including a lightning strike. They had, it seemed, already called in the local shaman and the Catholic priest to bless them. The women wept, asking forgiveness of each other and blessings from us. I asked them to bless me too: I was already uneasy at the imbalance between gringo and Indian. Ken was deferred to throughout as "Pastor" and we all sat on benches while the Indians sat on the ground. When we prayed, Stephen and I got off the bench to sit at their level.

> *The world awakes and is filled with light to worship thee,*
>   *O Creator of man.*
> *The lofty sky sweeps away her clouds in homage to thee, the*
>   *Maker of the world.*
> *The king of stars, Our Father, the sun, submits to thee his*
>   *power and might.*
> *The winds lift up the tops of the trees and wave each branch*
>   *in tribute to thee.*
> *From the shadowy woods the birds sing out to render praise*
>   *to the Ruler of all.*
> *The flowers show forth in brilliant array their vivid colours*
>   *and pungent perfumes.*
> *In the depths of the lake, in the watery world, the fish*
>   *proclaim their joy of thee.*
> *The dashing stream in bursting song exhausts in thee,*
>   *O Creator of man.*
> *The cliffs are dressed in glowing green, and the canyon walls*
>   *with flowers gleam.*
> *The serpents come from their forest abode to pay their*
>   *obedience due.*
> *The wary vicuña and shy viscacha [chinchilla] come down*

from the heights and are tame before thee. At the dawn
of day my heart sings praise to thee, my Father and
Creator of man.

Translation by Jesus Lara of an ancient poem, in
La Poesia Quechua y Aymara (Mexico: Fondo de
Cultura Economica, 1947), pp. 159–60

———

Over the border to Bolivia. Lake Titicaca was rough that day, and we were held up for four hours before being allowed to cross in life jackets handed out by members of the Bolivian navy. We had all got off our bus to board a small boat, and were astonished to see the buses being loaded on to rafts and being shipped across the lake. The sight of buses bobbing across the water was quite surreal.

> *Travelling along the highway some ten miles out of La Paz. A barren mountain landscape, no trees or grass, a small stream far below, very few cars on the road. From the bus we see a well kept dog on the roadside, looking up eagerly at our approach, left pathetically behind as we pass. A few minutes further on, another running out into the road behind us, a sad little figure receding into the distance. And another and another, every two hundred metres or so, spread out over an area of several miles: motley dogs, some terriers, some collies, mostly mongrels in varying degrees of dilapidation. Left without food on a bare mountainside by owners unwilling or unable to keep them. Left to die.*

We had arrived in Bolivia with no plans except to make contact with local Friends, particularly Jerry, a missionary friend of Ken and Tanya's who had indicated that he might have some work for us. We met him and his family at La Paz Friends church. Again the service lasted for three hours, a little boy in front of us helping us find the place in the Spanish/Aymara hymn book. As a theologian, Jerry was uneasy at the blurred distinctions between Quakers here and other evangelical churches, and frank in his admission that they had been good at evangelism but not at establishing Quakerism. He had not been able to find any work for us, but said that there was a Friends school in Coroico. We had already heard that Coroico was an attractive town and – most importantly – low enough to be warmer than La Paz, which, at over 3,600 metres (12,000 feet) is the highest capital in the world, and extremely cold at night. Unprepared for the temperature, I had caught a cold, and had to invest in an embroidered Bolivian jacket to keep warm in the evenings. Even so we found ourselves going to bed at about 8 p.m. just to get warm in our unheated hotel.

One day, walking along the street in La Paz, I felt myself splashed from above. I thought at first it was bird dropping, or water from a gutter, then found it was some unpleasant-smelling sticky substance that someone had thrown on me. As Stephen and I stopped to dab it off, two passers by stopped to help, proffering handkerchiefs. It was an unpleasant experience, and I was grateful for their solicitude. It was not till I saw one of them feeling in Stephen's bag that I realised it might be something else. Stephen felt one of them feeling in his pocket and whisked me away, saying, "Yes, thank you, thank you, we'll be fine now." Apparently it's a known scam; we had escaped lightly.

We were warned everywhere we went of theft and mugging, and heard terrible stories from some of the young travellers we met.

Endorsement on our Travelling Minute, La Paz

We carried very little money on us, keeping our moneybelts and other valuables locked in our cases when we were not on the move. We had, in any case, very little that was valuable with us, on the basis that we did not want to be worried about losing things. I had brought no jewellery and had not, though I was tempted, updated my very basic camera. Several times in South America we were stopped by passers by, telling us that a knapsack was undone and even once, in Rio, that the street we were on was not safe for foreigners. We left at once. We took care, and were not robbed in Latin America, or indeed at all until India. We did, however, lose things all the time, leaving hat or shampoo in a hotel bedroom or sunglasses on a bus. I think I got through four pairs in the year. Letting go.

The hotel in La Paz was situated in the middle of a giant market, spread all over this and neighbouring streets. Fruit, vegetables, piles and sacks of nuts and flour, hardware, fish and flowers. Patient Aymaran women with lined faces, large and voluminous in their many-layered clothing: billowing skirts, shawls and blankets, sitting, like their Quechua sisters in Peru, from early morning till after dark with their wares; then struggling on to our *collectivos* (shared taxis) with brilliant red stripey bundles, sometimes containing a baby, slung over their shoulders. The men were barely evident – perhaps because, not in costume, they blended into the background.

We ate in local cafés where the food was much the same as that which in Peru is called the "menu"; here, in Bolivia, it was known as the *almuerzo* (lunch) or *cena* (dinner). It was usually soup with a piece of meat and potato in a vegetable broth, followed by rice and potato with either fish or meat and sometimes a little (unsafe) salad. For about 50p it was perfectly satisfying. We never drank the water or ate unpeeled fruit or raw vegetables. A sad deprivation, but worth it in terms of our health.

We had not realised that altitude could make such a difference, and had become devotees of coca to deal with its effects. Though legal in South America, where coca tea is a common local drink, as the basis of cocaine it is illegal in most of the rest of the world and

Our bedroom: open to the Andes

the Americans are trying to get it banned in South America too. In Puno an interesting Italian woman doctor was running a café in a Franciscan mission; her passion was campaigning for the retention of coca. Few people seemed to smoke in South America, and it will be interesting to see how many people take it up if coca is banned. Certainly the advertising of the cigarette companies was very visible.

Coroico, nearly two thousand metres lower than La Paz but high enough to be above the mosquito line, sounded perfect. So we set off by bus – a literally breathtaking journey over mostly stony roads. A climb up to 4,800 metres, then a white knuckle hairpin ride down and down to 1,700 metres, from barren earth to semi-jungle. There were no barriers on the road, over the edge of which could be seen, some thousand metres below, several burnt-out wrecks of buses, to remind us of our possible fate. When a bus or car came the other way our bus drove on the wrong side of the road – to enable the driver to see the edge. It was that close. It was only afterwards that we discovered that the ride was known as the most dangerous bus journey in the world.

A mile or so outside the pretty town of Coroico we came across Sol y Luna and were captivated. Some six hectares, run by Sigrit, a German shiatsu exponent, as "a garden of the soul", it contained a central building with a pool, and self-catering cabins dotted around, out of sound and sight of each other. It was a perfect place to give each other some space and, crucially, opportunities for contemplation. Our *cabaña* with bamboo outbuildings of lavatory and shower was up some 95 steps and long slopes from the main house. It was open to the outside world on one side, with magnificent views of the mountains, high up in a land of birdsong, butterflies, soaring condors, squabbling green parrots and a myriad plants; a profusion of colour, texture and beauty.

The Friends school had closed for lack of funds. But we found the Friends, and met them for a service in a disused classroom with peeling walls. Though distant from our own silent worship, it was most touching. Seven people, mainly elderly and infirm, including one black woman who barely spoke Spanish, upholding their faith,

Stephen with Coroico Friends

singing in cracked voices, sometimes kneeling at the altar, sobbing out their prayers and confessions. They asked me (or rather, being a male-dominated culture, Stephen, who delegated to me) to read from the Bible. It was rather daunting, especially in Spanish, and I had no idea what was expected of me. Quakers of our "liberal" tradition revere the Spirit from which the Bible comes but do not treat it as the ultimate authority – only the direct experience of God is that. After a childhood of literal reading of the Bible, it is only recently that I have been able to return to it and appreciate its riches. On this occasion I played safe and read the 23rd Psalm.

The Coroico Friends agreed that we could use two classrooms of the defunct school to teach English. So we put a note up in the town square, offering lessons to all comers. I wrote in my journal on June 1st:

> *Life has begun to fall into place in a very pleasant simple practical way. Waking about 7 a.m. – the day starts late here with mist clearing from the mountains and valley very gradually though birds are busy long before. Woken in the night by a loud flapping that sounded in the room but was probably a bat trying to get through the zip-up sheet that Sigrit has erected to keep them out. Cup of tea in bed. Then breakfast – oats and apple, bread and honey, coffee; and domestic chores – washing, washing clothes – all in cold water, but with a good scrub board; sweeping up, emptying rubbish and burning some of it on the open fire we have outside. It is dusty here and damp – an odd combination. Then paperwork, reading, preparing for classes. Lunch – we take it in turns to cook – a nap and a swim. Down to town about 5.30 p.m. for shopping for the next day, internet sometimes, though it is very expensive, and teaching from 7 to 8.*

We had an average of about twenty pupils between us: Stephen ostensibly teaching the beginners (he has a TEFL qualification) and I the more advanced, but characteristically in a macho culture, the men all turned up for the advanced class; the women to the beginners. So Stephen had some bright young women in his class; I some completely uneducated old men, as well as young schoolboys and the local pharmacist, whose English was pretty good. They seemed hungry for knowledge but not eager to speak. One of the men had the name of Victor Hugo, another turned out to be Milton, and, not to be left out, the pharmacist said "and my name is William", obviously with Shakespeare in mind.

The only *amigo* (Quaker) in my class was a gentle young man of 22 who worked in the coffee fields between Coroico and La Paz, and steadily increased in confidence and articulateness as time went on. We had not realised that he was a Friend until he joined in our silent Meeting for Worship after class one day, together with the old *hermanos* (brothers) who didn't come to the classes but wanted to join with us in our kind of worship, as we had in theirs.

After class, Stephen and I went back to Sol y Luna either by a steep and scary walk past innumerable dogs in the dark (only torch or moonlight); or by taxi, to a light supper, a roaring fire and bed.

It was a good life that contained for us the right balance of meaningful work, self-sufficiency, the natural world and time for contemplation of it. The sight of the Andes dominated my awakening every morning, and penetrated my being. It was not prettiness but power. Not a dualistic admiration of something external but a call to something within me. I had felt it in the desert, and now it was as if a magnet had entered my soul.

CHAPTER 3

The Peacemakers

All bloody principles and practices we do utterly deny, with all outward wars, and strife, and fightings with outward weapons, for any end, or under any pretence whatsoever, and this is our testimony to the whole world.

Quaker declaration to Charles II, 1660

*C*osta Rica came as quite a surprise. After the magnificence of the Andes in Peru and Bolivia, it seemed tame, undramatic. Wonderfully green, but subtler and very evidently more affluent. I had wanted to begin our journey in North America and work south, feeling that we should start in more familiar territory and gradually progress to less familiar. It simply hadn't been possible in our juggling of timing, climate and mileage, but certainly my idea was borne out as the feeling of anticlimax grew.

Without the strong influence of Indian culture Costa Rica seemed an ethnically less interesting country. It is, however, unique in its progressive attitudes to war, thanks first to a constituent assembly which abolished the army in 1949 and then to Oscar Arias Sanchez, its president from 1986 to 1990, who was awarded the Nobel Peace Prize for his work on the Central American peace plan, which contributed so much to the ending of the continent's long-lasting civil wars.

When we arrived in San José, I was, for the first time, ill. Running out of Bolivian currency the previous night, we had wandered into the streets near our hotel in La Paz and, untypically, had eaten from a stall that looked dodgy. We had always been careful to eat freshly cooked food even in the most basic of places, but I knew in my heart that this was not safe – it was not even identifiable. Stephen took one mouthful then looked for somewhere to dispose of it, but I carried on eating. The result was a fearsome attack of diarrhoea early the next morning.

I sat at the airport feeling very unwell, and was approached several times by people asking if I wanted to see a doctor. In the end I agreed, then proceeded to vomit up the pill he had given me, resulting in an injection minutes before getting on the plane. Thankfully, I had three seats to myself and slept most of the way. When we arrived, the Bolivian prescription was hard to exchange in sophisticated San José.

The Costa Rican capital was more like a Western city than anything we had seen further south. A smart shopping area; all the goods one could buy in Europe; a homogenous white society. After nearly a week in the city, I couldn't wait to get out.

In Monteverde, in the north-west uplands, there is a well-established Quaker community, started by a group of American farmers at the time of the Korean war. Seeking respite from war-mongering, they found a land without an army, and have had a huge influence on the area. We were warmly welcomed into the community, and had our first unprogrammed Meeting for Worship for about two months, much needed. We visited the co-operative dairy and store, helped with the library and witnessed the expansion of the school and Meeting House. We also gave a talk on Quakerism at the Monteverde Institute, an establishment run by a Friend and concentrating on sustainable development and natural resource programmes. Students attend from all over the world – often for a term of their degree in architecture or land planning.

In general the town seemed expensive and disconcertingly unlike Latin America. Everyone, including the locals, spoke English and much had been provided for an American clientele. It is interesting how many people from developed countries seek their Shangri-la. In Brazil, our friends have bought a piece of paradise, having originally bought in southwest France, then moved on as life there became too sophisticated, too similar to what they were escaping from. But their patch of Brazil too has become expensive and exclusive as the incomers demand more sophisticated goods in the shops, even in the midst of a traditional fishing community. Then, in Coroico, Bolivia, Sigrid has successfully created a way of life that contributes to the wellbeing of those passing through and hopes to build a community, but it too is a thing apart from the context in which it exists. And here the advent of expats has resulted in a huge supermarket where you can find anything and a community that is quite separate from the rest of Costa Rica.

In all these places the new residents try to exploit their gifts – artistic for the most part, but also cooking and catering. Such communities employ local people and no doubt fit in well in some ways, but they do feel artificial implants that negate the reason for being there in the first place. In the end they permanently change the original environment – a concern that I know is held by some of the founding Quakers here.

Monteverde is primarily known for its cloud forest reserve, an area of high jungle rescued by the Quakers, who are still much involved in the administration of what has become a major attraction of ecotourism. At 6 a.m. one day we were able to walk for four hours in the 10,500 hectare reserve, among the giant trees. We were soon out of sight and sound of other people, and revelling in the misty lush foliage dripping with the low cloud, and the sound, and occasionally sight, of bell birds and howling monkeys.

Lord, make me an instrument of thy peace

St Francis of Assisi

Spiritually our time in Costa Rica was dominated by encounters with two men in San José – one Costa Rican, one American; both Quakers who live their faith. The peace testimony is central to Quaker beliefs, so it is not surprising that they, like Arias, live lives directed towards peace.

Arriving by bus in the downtown area of Desamparados in San José, we were astonished to find the small unpretentious houses barricaded with bars. As we walked down the road, we passed people sitting in their front yard or porch behind bars, like animals in a zoo. We had come across rich homes in Lima, Peru similarly fortified, but in this modest area the fear of crime was unexpected and shocking.

Napoleon and Clothilde Escobar live in a small self-built house with a corrugated roof, together with their son and girlfriend. Both

Servas members and Quakers, they were a natural choice for us as hosts, and indeed our couple of days with them were a source of richness. Napoleon has trained in the Alternatives to Violence Project (AVP): a scheme set up by Quakers in American prisons in the 1970s that attempts to build self-esteem and inculcate skills in dealing with anger and preventing conflict. With no financial support and little evidence of any income at all, Napoleon and Clothilde run peace workshops, based on AVP, mainly for drug addicts, with considerable success. With pride they showed us their scrapbooks, and copies of the certificates they give to those who have participated.

Another Servas member was *in situ* at the Escobars' house. Martin, a young German forester, who had been due to leave some days before, had had to stay on for treatment for a painful abscess at the local hospital. Since there are only two bedrooms in the house – one for Napoleon and Clothilde, the other for their son and his girlfriend ("They stay up late studying") – and Martin was established on the sitting room sofa, we asked tentatively where we should put our rucksacks.

"Oh, in here" – pointing to the master bedroom.

"Oh, no, we couldn't possibly," but

"Oh, we'll be in there too" – and they moved the mattress off the bed.

We slept on the mattress, Napoleon and Clothilde on the base, and the dog and cat at our feet, a perfect warm, loving and cosy arrangement. It was one of many lessons about different attitudes to privacy.

And such generosity. We had home-made bread every morning. The first night their son cooked pasta for us all. The second I cooked a fish pie (finding prawns was impossible – no one in the local shops knew even the Spanish word for prawn so I had to give up on them). I also sang for my hosts – an increasingly common way for me to "pay" for my keep. I have sung all my life, mainly opera and lieder, but I was limited on the trip by what I knew by heart, and by what seemed appropriate to my audience. In general I sang traditional folk songs which do not suffer from being unaccompanied and are generally accessible, although I occasionally allowed myself the expansive pleasure of the operatic repertoire.

Napoleon, a member of the local Quaker Meeting, was estranged from it, ironically in an argument over AVP. Peacemaking seems to throw up these tensions: there was a similar conflict among Servas members in Peru. We were touched when he and Clothilde, who had never joined Quakers, asked if they could come to Meeting with us on Sunday. Martin too came, for his first Quaker Meeting, and the usually small group was further amplified by the presence of two other visitors to the town. It was held, as usual, in the San José Quaker Peace Center, and was a profoundly moving occasion. The talk that Stephen and I gave, on social action and mysticism, seemed to go down well and was interpreted for Clothilde, who speaks no English.

In the evening, Clothilde asked about applying for membership of the Religious Society of Friends, and Stephen sat down and explained the simple procedure, giving her an informal interview in the process. If our presence acted as a catalyst, we will be content.

———

The Clerk of the Meeting was Diego Low, a small, bearded, intense American. He was also the recently appointed director of the Peace Center, so active as a base for reconciliation during the war years of the 1980s but now seeking new directions. Before coming to Costa Rica Diego had spent many years in the States doing human rights work with undocumented workers, mainly Mexicans. His paid job when we met him was in an organisation seeking justice for workers in Costa Rica, particularly women, in the new free trade zones, which in general repress union activity and have worse working conditions than elsewhere.

We had arrived in San José with no plans, just a wish to be useful. We did not have the skills to slot into any particular project, but, in discussion with Diego, we all felt that perhaps we could simply bear witness, visit projects, inform ourselves and report back. Diego, so well connected in the field of human rights, took us in hand.

Diego Low

It was by now the rainy season; the weather stiflingly hot and humid as we drove down to the Caribbean coast. We stayed right on the shore, near the village of Puerto Uva, in a house belonging to the boss of Diego's *compañera*, Ileana. A large wooden house with magnificent verandas in the midst of tropical jungle, it had possibly the greatest range of animal life of our whole journey. On June 27th, I wrote in my journal:

The richness of the wildlife is overwhelming – some less welcome than others, like the numerous biting insects and ants that sting you as you lean up against a door post, the large spider that eases itself into the kitchen, even the "esperanza", the huge leaf-like grasshopper that hurtled across the kitchen on to a plastic bag this morning. The bats hanging from the bathroom eaves, red crabs and some pale blue ones crawling out from under the hedges and into holes all round the garden, lizards darting out into the sun, staying just ahead of us on the path to the beach, the roar of howling monkeys from nearby trees. A blue morpho butterfly yesterday and a lovely blue and yellow one today. Most of all the birds, both in tantalising song and also

visually:"pechos amarillos" [yellow breasts] of many varieties; the fleeting
glimpse of a woodpecker, the stillness of perched vultures, the startling red of
the back of a black bird sitting close to the house in front of flowers of exactly
the same hue, hummingbirds and many other tiny birds, perching, singing,
darting from tree to tree. And the foliage of every imaginable shape, size and
shade of green. Humid, rainy, itchy, but nature in all its splendour.

From here Diego took us to visit some projects to which he was offering support.

Foro Emaus is a group of churches, non-governmental organisations (NGOs), trade unions and academics set up 'for Human Rights and the Environment' mainly in the banana industry, trying to get the corporations to accept minimum standards of employment. International markets, especially the USA, demand standard products, in this case, long straight bananas, and there is a terrible wastage of any that do not conform.

Abuses of human rights and the land are well documented, especially in the use of pesticides. These not only desolate the land, making it impossible for further use after cropping, but have also affected the fertility of a high proportion of men who had worked in the local banana industry. In discussions at the local banana packing factory, managers assured us of improved conditions and said that some of the worst pesticides were no longer used. The union leaders did not dispute these statements, though they also spoke of victimisation of women and some of their own officials. The workers are mostly immigrants and indigenous Indians, who live with their families in barrack-like living quarters near the factory. The lively co-operative of small independent farmers producing organic bananas was a contrast. An organisation of equals, it strives to make a living from its produce, most of which is made into a famous brand of baby food.

Costa Rica has a complex and inconsistent attitude towards its borders. In the border town of Sixaola no one minded Stephen and me walking across the rickety wooden bridge into Panama: people came and went from both sides, to school and to work. Very different was the attitude to Nicaraguans, large numbers of whom are driven by

A banana packing factory

poverty to try to find a better life in Costa Rica – many of the banana workers, for instance, are illegal immigrants.

But it's the Colombians who cause the most anxiety, as a dramatic event on our doorstep demonstrated. Early one morning there were alarums and excursions as the police discovered a large boat on the beach near the house. It wasn't clear whether it had carried immigrants or drug smugglers, though we later discovered that our guard/caretaker had appropriated two barrels from the site of we knew not what. We went out to watch police photographing clothes and a mobile phone recovered from the boat, but only on return to San José did we hear that the TV news had reported a seizure of cocaine.

In Sixaola we were welcomed by the Baptist pastor and local human rights activist, Enrique de la O, who showed us round his parish. On our last day, we met Erlinda, a women's rights worker, active in the banana business and trying to find local women alternative

48

employment. She was interested in the flexibility that self-employment offers to women with children, and we discussed the possibility of setting up a microcredit project. On our way back to town we were held up for two hours by *campesinos* demonstrating for higher prices for their goods. Some had been there all night. We were alarmed to see police with riot shields and tear gas, but after some lively negotiation all passed peacefully.

Costa Rica is at the forefront of ecological awareness in Central America. There was considerable anger and anxiety about plans for oil rigs being set up yards off the beautiful Caribbean shore. A committee of Accion de Lucha Anti-petrolera (ADELA) had been set up to represent the interests of local people and 40 local NGOs. Informed by previous experience, particularly in Mexico, they were worried about oil spillage, and the effect of drills on the beaches, and of detonation on the fish. There had been little local consultation before an agreement had been signed giving a 20-year lease with complete rights and no protective measures to combat possible environmental effects. There were no guarantees about possibly disastrous effects on the air, the water or the health of local residents. The government, which had signed joint ventures, was proposing the drilling as a solution to the considerable economic problems of the area – producing jobs and an oil-rich economy. The reality was that the project would only result in about 60 jobs, of which 60% would be given to outside specialists and the remainder would be "dirty" jobs. Previous experience showed that the project would also result in drink and prostitution. ADELA felt that their most powerful argument was that the proposed drilling would adversely affect the ecological tourism for which Costa Rica is increasingly known and which economically is as important for the country as coffee and bananas. They wanted to keep the country free of oil exploration, and for Costa Rica to become the leader in a new era of exploration of alternative energy.

With each group of campaigners Diego was able to offer use of the Peace Center as a resource, usefully near government offices and courts in the capital. It was, as Stephen later wrote, "truly inspiring to witness the influence that a few people, allowing themselves to be led by the Spirit, and willing to speak truth to power, can have on the politics and economy of their country." I found Diego a kindred spirit, with whom I could discuss the problems of discernment and ways forward on our spiritual paths. He was at a crossroads: feeling a call but tied by personal commitments.

On our return to San José, we accepted Diego's invitation to stay with him and his family. He shares his house with Ileana, her parents and her sister's three children. A large horizontal building in a rural setting outside the city, it is divided in two parts with a covered courtyard in the middle. He was concerned that we might find their haphazard lifestyle difficult. We reassured him that nothing would please us more, but I confess that we were not prepared for the six dogs of varying shapes and sizes that met us with frenzied barks of welcome.

It was a warm rumbustious household, generous and loving. Another example of the ministry of hospitality that we encountered all over the world. On the day we left, having decided to forgo our flight to Honduras, taking the overland bus through Nicaragua instead, Diego saw us off, at 4.30 a.m.! A ministering angel, he had facilitated nearly everything that we had done in Costa Rica.

In the tradition of Arias, as we saw in the lives of both Napoleon and Diego, the job of peacemaking goes on.

CHAPTER 4

Doing the Splits

We have a variety of strategies for passing by on the other side: we manage not to know about such things, by living elsewhere and averting our eyes and hearts from information which might trouble us.

Jonathan Dale, in *Quaker Faith and Practice*

After Costa Rica, the poverty of Nicaragua and Honduras was shocking. We had not intended to go to Nicaragua – I had what turned out to be an outdated concern about safety – but, hearing from fellow travellers of how much they had enjoyed it, we cancelled our flight to Honduras, and decided to travel overland instead.

For once Stephen was in agreement about not spending much time in the capital. Managua is a sad and sprawling city that has been decimated by earthquake, fire, revolution and the flooding that resulted from Hurricane Mitch in 1998. Not generally nervous in city streets, Stephen felt quite unsafe as he went on a long expedition on foot the evening we were there to try to find a bank that would take Mastercard. We stayed overnight at the Quaker hostel, in order to attend Meeting for Worship at the small worship group of unprogrammed Friends that meets in the peace centre. Sadly, the clerk was absent, no one knew how to contact the others, and there was no Meeting. After a plastic pastry breakfast in a mostly shut shopping precinct, we held a Meeting for Worship on our own in the lobby of the hostel. It was the rainy season, and we were soaked as we left our hotel to seek out lunch in the empty streets. Nothing local to be found.

Throughout South and Central America we had been warned that bus stations were dens of iniquity. By hanging on to our possessions and not wandering about at night, we had not had any problems, but at the bus station in Managua we witnessed an ugly punch-up between one of the officials and a rather pathetic homeless man who had simply got in the way. The same aggressive official touched up one of the young women vendors as she passed – no doubt part of the trials of her daily life.

Granada, our next stop, was a charming colonial town with a lovely main square. On this steamy Sunday it was full of local people, relaxing in the cafés, and on benches among the trees. We sat with cold drinks, taking in the sights. The strange sight of a self-conscious young tourist, a very tall man wearing a quite outlandish stetson, walking back and forth across the square. The unbelievable sight, too far across the square, of a young boy on crutches arguing with his father who took off his belt, and there in public, in front of us all, whipped him. No one said or did a thing, but the boy, now cowed and crying, followed his parents out of the square.

The hotel we were staying in was pretty basic: a square of buildings round a garden festooned with washing. One night we arrived back from supper after 9.30 p.m. to find it shut up. We had to wake up the thin little girl – a drudge of not more than 16 – to let us in. In the garden the next morning a middle-aged woman was sitting on a chair, listless and alone. She was a German tourist, and she was very ill. The reason for her permanent diarrhoea was being investigated by the rather basic local hospital, but she had been unable to eat for days, and was now far too weak to travel to the capital where the medical facilities might be better. I talked to her for a while, offered to shop for her if necessary. Why did we not stay to take care of her, take her to Managua? Too much in a hurry, as usual; against all our intentions, we were on a schedule.

Finca Magdalena is a co-operative farm on Omatepe, the largest island on a freshwater lake in the world (our journey was peppered with these *Guinness Book of Records* entries). We had reached the island by a four-hour boat journey, sitting on the deck among a pleasant group of young tourists and local people. When we arrived at a small pier, with no town in sight, we confidently sat on, having been told it would be another hour. By the time we realised that this was our stop, most people had left, and oncomers were flowing in with their sacks and cases over the single plank to the land. We struggled ashore to find the bus gone, and only a truck taxi available. It was the first time I had travelled standing up in the back of a truck, and I found the two-kilometre ride exhilarating, sweeping through the luxuriant foliage, we ducking to miss low branches in the cool night air.

The following day we caught a rickety bus along a potholed dirt track to Balgue, from where a 1,300-metre track uphill led us to the farm. It was the first time we had actually had to carry our rucksacks, and in the heat the effort was shattering.

The finca was a ranch, and for the first time we saw horses used as a matter of course, ridden with aplomb and without a saddle. It was a lovely place, with howling monkeys and long-tailed white-breasted birds in the trees, an extinct volcano rising up behind us. Groups of fit young people would go up in the early morning with a guide and reappear in mid-afternoon, muddy and exhausted. The farm also provided a hostel, in a large subdivided barn, with simple showers at one end. There was no light in the loos; torches were as usual a necessity. A large toad near the entrance watched us come and go.

The finca was a restful place with hammocks, tables and chairs on a large open veranda on which we and the many young visitors sat, conversed, slept and read, gazing out over the large lake at the bottom of the hill. People were working in the fields around, chopping weeds with a machete – all the men and many of the small boys carried them – building a home, planting sunflower seeds and, in the house, cooking for us all. We had hoped to do some voluntary work, but it didn't materialise, though Stephen did help a bit with carrying stones. We heard that Westerners were pretty useless at cutting cane or picking coffee, so presumably it wasn't worth asking us.

The finca was one of the few remaining co-operative farms in the country, flourishing because they had found a Canadian market for their coffee. The owners were Sandinistas, supporters of the governing party brought down by the Contras and an American blockade in the 1980s. Workers on the farm during the civil war, they had been granted the farm by the communists who had wrested it from an absentee landlord. While we were there, we joined them to watch some of the party political broadcasts for the Sandinista candidate in the forthcoming elections. Generally the TV was only on for the daily soap, to which the staff were addicted – with melodramatic stock villains, heroes and heroines. The farm had no manager, but was run collectively, each member taking a role. Stephen questioned them at some length, with me attempting to interpret, because it turned out that they had solved the question of inheritance, which a similar Quaker-run farm we had come across in Costa Rica was finding it hard to deal with. Stephen passed the information on, hoping that in acting as a conduit for such information, we were serving a useful purpose.

We climbed for an hour up the volcano, but we were neither young nor with a guide, so it was not surprising that we got lost in the jungle. The path petered out in the dense foliage, and we were content to come down, stopping halfway to sit and look at the butterflies – twelve different varieties within minutes. On our way down we encountered a man with a machete who had been working in the fields. I engaged him in conversation, Stephen not feeling his Spanish was up to it, and since I was doing all the talking, the man started to make false assumptions, and asked me more personal questions. Noting Stephen's bald head and the fact he was older than me, the man asked if he was rich. I cottoned on at last, and made my excuses.

The village at the bottom of the hill was small and straggling with a few shops and houses with porches serving as cafés, both stocking little other than the ubiquitous Coca-Cola. We occasionally bought some to be sociable, but in general I preferred to drink bottled water. Little home industries were visible from the road, including a machine we passed in an open yard. Stephen felt it looked familiar and discovered that, yes, it was a Petter engine, made many years before by his father's family, shipped out here, and now used for milling rice.

The magnificent crested birds I had seen earlier turned out to be local magpies – why should I have felt disappointed? Their beauty was unchanged. In the pre-dawn, I was woken by a cacophony of howling monkeys, parrots and the alarm calls of various birds.

It was hard to leave, but the time had come to move on to Honduras and Guatemala, where my mother and daughter, Juliet, were waiting for us.

We were getting used to the complexities of crossing the borders in Central America, though we still succumbed to swindling on occasions. The tricycle taxi that we had hired to take us over the border between Nicaragua and Honduras, waiting with our luggage as we fulfilled the bureaucratic procedures in leaving one country and entering another, was driven by a past master. Despite a tip for his patience given before we were through, the young man still tried to assert that the price he had quoted was in dollars, not pesos. We stood firm, but as always the attempt left a sour taste.

Because of our decision to travel through Nicaragua, we now only had a week in Honduras, and no plans except to visit Tela, on the Caribbean coast, which Stephen had visited some years before for an international Quaker conference.

Our first stop, which proved not to be on the way to our destination, was a characterless little town called San Marcos en Colon, but it was at least higher up, and cooler. It took four bus journeys in one day to get there, all quite smoothly connected, apart from the tussle at the border. Although we were well under budget at this point, we were chronically short of ready cash, scrabbling around for meals, as it was so difficult to find places to draw it.

One of the four journeys was a classic: vastly overcrowded, often four to a seat that comfortably seated two in one of those long yellow ex-US school buses that are so prevalent in Central America. The number and variety of vendors on board were prodigious – one man pronouncing for about ten minutes on the virtues of a protein food. There were sellers of sweets, bags of water, plantain crisps, toys and various other foods, the women vendors unable to squeeze past all the standing passengers.

Our stay in San Marcos was in an unfriendly place which made us pay in advance. Despite treating us with complete indifference, the owners were obviously "religious", as there were Biblical quotations all over the walls. There was also one saying, "Do not spit on the walls" and Stephen, a child at heart, climbed up and wrote in pencil, "Only on the floor". An odd noise came and went throughout the night, like a bird – three whistled notes. It turned out to be a watchman patrolling with a big stick and blowing a whistle. And when we arrived in Tela we met the local equivalent: a nice elderly man carrying a sword! Yes, he said, he was a watchman, a vigilante.

We had telephoned a few days earlier to "book" a Servas host in Tela, and we arrived by bus at night. In the dark it was hard for the taxi to find the way but we finally realised that her address was not near "Boardinghouse Sara" but actually in it.

Our hostess, Alma, had inherited the three-storeyed rickety edifice from her parents who had run it as a boarding house for some 30 years. The attractive wooden construction was thoroughly dilapidated, and impossible to operate as a commercial concern. To our embarrassment we learnt that Alma had resigned from Servas as she could not afford to keep people there for free, but she would not hear of any payment from us. She lived there with an extended family that we never quite got the hang of, and was looking to sell. We promised to help her advertise, perhaps in the States – for the place had potential – but she never followed up with the details.

The house was almost on the beach, with just a row of down at heel little shacks between us and the sea. From our room we could see the inhabitants at their daily chores, filling buckets with water, washing in the yard. The beach itself was grubby and unappealing and the whole area demonstrated the poverty of a country where there is nearly 50% unemployment. Along the road passed horses and carts, one carrying a motor bike, and even at 7 a.m. drunken men were zigzagging from the drinking den on the beach, round the corner. It was an unattractive place, with broken glass all around and stray dogs wandering the streets.

Dogs were quite a feature of our journey. To begin with, rabies in mind, I was terrified of all the stray dogs; after a while they seemed a commonplace; always several wandering around. Some were pets, but two of the most unpleasant things we saw centred round dogs. One was the abandonment of dogs in Bolivia; the other an incident here in Honduras, when we saw a wraith-like dog in the street, obviously near death, being stoned by a little girl to keep it away from her pet. How could a child be taught to be so kind to one dog and so cruel to another?

From our end of town – the old part – Tela was a sad place. Further up, the town was bustling, with cafés and restaurants aimed at the tourists. In fact it was hard to find a local place open, though we frequented a café that did very good fruit juice, except when the power failed. We wandered up the beach one day to see the conference complex at which Stephen had stayed some 15 years before: very smart, and in a different world from Boardinghouse Sara. The great divide again.

On the way to Tela, Stephen divulged another reason for wanting to go to that part of Honduras. It was rather a romantic story. While at the conference, the delegates had been taken to a nearby village called Triunfo de la Cruz, a Garifuna village. The Garifuna are black, quite unlike the rest of the inhabitants of Central America, and are the descendants of escaped slaves who had been deported from St Vincent in the eighteenth century and dumped by the British on the coast of Central America. They retain their own culture and language and have, naturally enough, a reserve towards white people.

Some years after his visit, Stephen had read in the British papers of the devastation of the village by Hurricane Mitch, and of a teacher from the little school in the village who had been picked up by a British vessel some 20 miles off the coast. Stephen was keen to visit the village, and see if we could perhaps help in the school. So we took the bus five kilometres up the coast to Triunfo de la Cruz, and asked for the school. When we arrived, it was no little shack but a large modern comprehensive. We were taken aback and somewhat embarrassed, as no one seemed to understand my explanation in limited Spanish of

Garifuna children

why we were there. Finally, a more senior teacher arrived and we were able to make ourselves understood.

"Oh," said he, "that's quite another village, fifty miles up the coast." In our ignorance, we had not realised that there are many Garifuna villages, dotted along the coasts of Honduras, Belize, Nicaragua and Guatemala.

But we were so taken with the place that we decided to stay anyway. The last bus had left at 4.30 p.m. – it seemed that the Garifuna, many of whom commuted to work in Tela, had no way out after that hour – so we were lucky to get a taxi. We had to wait a while for it, and noticed a decided antipathy from some of the locals standing around at the corner where we were waiting. Stephen was all for walking the mile or so to the main road to hitch a lift but, for once, I didn't feel altogether safe. Once in Tela, we left our rucksacks with Alma, taking only a bag each, and the next day went back to Triunfo and installed ourselves in a grass hut on the beach for a week.

What a difference five kilometres makes. For Triunfo was lovely. Just how I imagined the Caribbean – clear warm sea, pale sand, rush shelters to protect us from the sun, few tourists, local people who were on the whole friendly, and grilled fish on the beach (though the cook had to take it out of the freezer – nothing's perfect). We made friends with some of the children, who were already well aware of financial realities. One, a delightful little girl of about four whose pretend food I pretended to sample and pay for, gave me my pretend change with great seriousness. Also serious was an older girl who asked if I would like to have my hair plaited, like her sister's. Pointing at my extremely short white hair, I asked if she thought it worth it, but she did. It was apparent that this was a business transaction, so I asked her how much she wanted. After a grave conversation in Garifuna with her younger sister she named a pretty outrageous sum. I suggested a lesser amount, and she seemed to agree. After the work, she showed me the rather odd result in the mirror; I expressed pleasure, and paid her. She seemed crestfallen, and I realised that what she had said was that I could have a partial job, and if I liked it I could pay more for the rest.

A pair of Stephen's trousers were stolen off the bush on which he had put them to dry overnight – very tiresome, as they were the

Paradise!

only pair of long trousers he had brought with him. Our landlord was concerned and tried to help, but there was nothing to be done. We built up a good relationship with him: he put a hammock up for me and tried to curb the high-decibel music issuing from the barn-like structure near by. We also got on well with the very dignified cook a bit further down the beach, whose husband had gone on a fishing trip for three days; she unbent as we returned to sample her fare on several occasions. When we were hungry, we would wander barefoot along the sand with our torches, give our order and return an hour later to sit at a wooden table outside her hut in the dark, often with her daughter who did not speak to us, but concentrated on her homework.

The Garifuna are poor. Not only, in practice, does the lack of transport subject them to a curfew, but they also lack most of the amenities available in the predominantly Latin town of Tela. We shopped at the local stalls but had to go into town to use the phone.

We learnt more about the Garifuna from the local museum, where we saw something of their craft work, and learnt of their closeness to the land, which like Native Americans they believe may not be bought or sold, their tight-knit family relationships and their belief in the unity of all creation. They had brought much of their culture and religious ceremonies from the West Indies, including a precursor of rock and roll and a special kind of dancing for Christmas. But we simply weren't there long enough to penetrate their society for ourselves.

———

Living simply was at the heart of my vision for the journey. Quakers have a testimony to simplicity: we believe it is important to remove the clutter that distances us from our relationship with God. More relevantly, perhaps, we also have a testimony to equality: the belief that all people are equal, that we do not treat anyone differently, so travelling on local transport, in touch with local conditions, was for me a crucial factor.

On the whole we have managed to escape the affluence of our usual environment. We travel on local buses, eat in small local cafés, stay in backpackers' hotels. We are – at 54 and 64 – invariably the oldest travellers: a source of curiosity, I think, to our companions in their gap year or taking a break before "settling down". It has not in any sense felt a duty. Travelling for a year, funded by the rent from our flat, we have to watch our expenditure, but more importantly travelling in this way is what we enjoy. I don't feel we are roughing it. Places are basic but clean; food is at the very least "interesting". Buses, if cramped, are a hive of activity and bustling with local culture.

The one occasion when we were forced to go on a luxury bus at three times the ordinary fare, we were surrounded by tourists, deafened by a violent American video, and made sick by the over-soft suspension and the smell of the non-functioning chemical lavatory.

This was written after nearly three months in Latin America – the first three months of our trip. It was basic living that I had enjoyed hugely. At the end of that three months we left Honduras to go to Guatemala for a family reunion at the house of my Guatemalan cousin, Christy – and everything changed.

Our journey from Honduras to Guatemala was one of the few bad journeys of our entire year. The previous day we had been told that there was a train three times a week from Tela to Puerto Cortes. After travelling over a continent without trains we were delighted at the prospect, and had set off to catch it, only to find that we had been misinformed. After crossing into Guatemala by a series of exorbitant *colectivos*, and charged an entry fee that we later realised was illegal, we were advised that we could catch our bus to Guatemala City at the crossroads. We stood with others in the baking heat, thirst quenched by produce from a stall piled high with pineapples, skilfully peeled with a few deft chops of a knife and cut in half, with the stalk left on as a handle.

At noon I phoned Christy to say that we were on our way. As I phoned, the first of several buses sped past without stopping and, finally, a passer by told us that no buses would stop there; we needed to go into town to book seats on these very popular buses. There we discovered the next bus to Guatemala City was not for another two hours. Having just crossed the border, we had only the small amount of Guatemalan money that we had received for our Honduran notes until we could get to a bank the next day. Saving enough money for the bus from Guatemala City to our destination, Antigua, we bought a little food and settled down to wait. In the meantime we got chatting to a young man who turned out to be a born again Christian. A delightful man, he shared with us some aspects of his Bible-centred faith.

When we finally boarded the bus and got a few miles past where we had been waiting earlier, it burst a tyre, twice. On the first occasion the tyre was changed; on the second we had to wait for three hours, sitting on the roadside, until a replacement arrived. By this time we had got to know our fellow passengers pretty well. Just as well, as we finally arrived in Guatemala City at 10 p.m., after the last bus to Antigua had left, and with no money for a taxi.

Guatemala City is not a place to be in, or rather, out in, at night. I have never been in a city so deserted at 10 p.m. Not a person on the dark streets, as we sped along one after another. Alighting, we saw one sinister-looking hotel, and thought with sinking hearts that that would be our only possibility. But our new-found friends came to our aid. One had a mobile phone which I borrowed to phone Christy, who of course said she would lend us the money for our taxi; the other haggled with the taxi driver; and we were able to give a free lift to our young companions. On the way I thoroughly enjoyed the theological discussion between our young Christian friend and the taxi driver, though my Spanish was not good enough to join in.

All this time we had been, of course, travelling rough, mucking in, the only foreigners on the trip. We had spent the previous night in hammocks hung over an open-sided platform, were strapped for cash, and marooned in Guatemala City without enough money to get by. When our taxi driver finally found Christy's house, and the door opened to reveal a palatial establishment, our young companions were dumbfounded, their astonishment writ large on their faces. What on earth, we could imagine them saying, as they turned to go, were those people doing? Middle-aged people with such rich relations. Why did they make us believe they had nothing?

Almost impossible to answer, and it made me feel a fraud. All my ideals of simple travelling were dashed at a stroke; my pretence of living alongside poor people revealed as an idealistic mirage.

Can we truly live with the poor? . . . Some say that to be a priest to the poor you should be no different from them, others say that is not realistic or even authentic.

Henri Nouwen

My discomfort continued for much of the time that we were in Guatemala.

Of course it was wonderful to be welcomed, enfolded in soft beds and – oh, luxury – the first bath for three months! And lovely to see Christy and my mother and daughter who had flown over to be with us. The house, in Christy's family for several generations, takes up a block of the city, and is very beautiful. Essentially L-shaped, it has an outdoors corridor with hanging baskets full of orchids – Christy is a collector. Each room is exquisitely furnished; all the rooms with bathroom en suite, and the grounds extensive and beautifully landscaped. Together with her French husband (my mother's cousin), they lived in Paris for many years, and came back to Guatemala on retirement to spend time with Christy's children. So much of the taste is French; the books a mixture of English, French and Spanish.

Antigua is an elegant eighteenth-century town; its low pastel-painted houses have escaped the earthquake desolation of other cities in the area. My time there in many ways passed very pleasantly, in walking, sightseeing, catching up with emails, shopping and spending time with my family. We ate extraordinarily well and were looked after. Christy and I went visiting and went to a trio recital in an elegantly restored old building. She introduced us to her friends and held a delightful bridge evening at which I sang the "Seguidilla" and "Habañera" from *Carmen* – my favourite role in the mezzo repertoire.

Stephen and I were invited to tea by a retired American diplomat whom Stephen had met in the bank queue, an expat of considerable standing. He lived in the same road as Christy, in a house that abutted on to the ruins of a seventeenth-century church – a highly original residence that he had inhabited for 45 years. He said he expected an earthquake soon, but seemed quite phlegmatic about it. He and a friend who dropped in were full of horror stories about violence and robberies. On my previous visit to Christy, her friends told me of the kidnapping of other friends' children; most had armed guards around their properties. Not surprising in a country with a repressive right-wing regime; a country with so many "disappeareds", oppression, violence and fear: the hallmarks of a divided country. Fifteen years on, though the political situation seemed to have improved, the poverty was still extreme.

Our time in Antigua was very pleasant – the kind of middle-class lifestyle that is familiar to many of my friends in England. But I felt the need to shrink the social, expand the spiritual. It was a strong force in me now. Being in an ashram for a few days, which was Stephen's dream, was for me an artificial break. I wanted more silence and solitude in my normal life.

At the service at the Friends church in Guatemala City, we were particularly struck by the fact that the three people on the platform were women. We spoke to one of them afterwards as she gave us a lift to the bus station. She explained that she was training to be a pastor, but with three children it was a slow job. Her father is a pastor, and he has educated her in Quaker history – he has attended a Quaker conference in Britain. As a result, she knew all about our tradition of worship, and confided that she would prefer it – "We have no time to listen to God". She hoped that they might soon include some silence in their Meetings. Also unusually, the sermon (delivered by a man) referred to social issues such as racism, and to mentions of "the Light" and "the Spirit", differentiating the Quaker faith from that of other denominations. Of all the evangelical services we attended, this came closest to our own way of looking at things. There is, apparently, a group of unprogrammed Friends in Antigua but it meets only fortnightly, and we missed it.

To be in a house with servants, food served, any item of clothing dropped on the floor arriving the next morning, washed and ironed, was so different from what we had grown used to in the rest of Latin America: our meals of a big bowl of soup for thirty pence; cold water to wash in; and lavatories of the most basic kind. It does show a measure of adaptability that we could so easily inhabit different parts of the planet but I could not forget my unease at being so removed from the life of the country.

It was a time for reflection, writing and reading that we badly needed, but I felt a dis-comfort, an un-ease. In my emails to friends I struggled to explain my response: it was not a rationalised or willed feeling that this way of life was inappropriate but just where I seemed – rather to my surprise – to be. I felt that I was again allowing my life to become disjointed, that I was in the wrong place. When we got on a bus to go to a Friends church in Guatemala City, squashed up against breastfeeding mothers and market traders, the radio seemingly stuck on the same tune we had heard in buses all over Latin America, I felt again at ease, content, at unity with those around me. I had forgotten what I had written on the eve of departure about trying to get away from "the spoilt affluence of this part of the world" but it was obviously a feeling that ran deep.

It had become clear that for me the driving force behind the trip was a need to live a life more in touch with how others live. Having left the "glamorous" profession of publishing after thirty years because I felt increasingly out of kilter with the prevailing mores, I seemed in the previous three years to have moved into a different place. I no longer felt I belonged in the world of publishing, or even in the world of some of my own relations. We had started this trip with a two-week "holiday" in the luxurious seaside home of a publishing friend in Brazil – completely idyllic, but we had felt an impatience to get on with the trip proper. And now with three months of that "trip proper" behind us, it was all the more difficult to fit in with a life that seemed to belong to my past.

Obras Sociales del Hermano Pedro: children's ward

A slight intimation of the poverty that had been surrounding us in Guatemala came from the week I spent as a volunteer in the children's ward of a charity hospital. Walking one day into what I thought was part of a church, I found the notice: "There are 500 patients in this hospital: 175 have been abandoned." On the spur of the moment I asked if any would like to be visited, thinking my Spanish would be up to holding someone's hand for an hour or so. They asked if I would like to volunteer, and to my surprise, after my family had left, I found myself working for the Obras Sociales del Hermano Pedro.

I hadn't had much to do with small children since my own were that age, but I found myself increasingly involved: feeding the little premature baby from a bottle, cuddling little two-year-olds, playing with older ones, and the ones in wheelchairs, some very badly disabled. Apart from other medical problems, all the children were severely malnourished, with the result in some cases that they had not the strength to cough hard enough to clear their congestion. Many were running temperatures, and had to be thumped and their noses drained every day. To put up with so much when so little; no wonder they needed cuddling. I found it hard to remember the names of the children, but I soon realised it was because no one used them. Apparently, names are not really given to children under the age of five, so that the evil spirits have less to get hold of.

There were several other foreign volunteers, including an American physiotherapist who gave the wheelchair-bound children a lot of pleasure; indeed the ward seemed quite well served. But the children needed our care. The staff were overworked, and many of the children barely saw their parents, who lived in distant villages without the money to visit. Several cried piteously for their mothers. One, to whom I paid a lot of attention, cried every time I put her down, and it tore at my heart. But they were not the only needy ones. Downstairs there was a ward of adolescents: mainly severely disabled. They truly seemed abandoned, all in identical clothing, sitting staring for long hours, or waving their arms and uttering guttural sounds of frustration. No volunteers seemed to be working there, but I did not feel up to the task. To my shame I chickened out, but when I left the hospital after the week, glad that I had not stayed long enough for the children to get attached to me, it was I who found myself in tears.

Travelling Hopefully

This we know. The earth does not belong to man; man belongs to the earth.
This we know. All things are connected like the blood that unites one family.
All things are connected . . . Our God is the same God. The earth is precious to
him. Even the white man cannot be exempt from the common destiny. We may
be brothers after all. We shall see.

Words by Ted Perry, based on Chief Seattl's speech
to the President of the United States in 1854

*I*had a real problem with being in first-world countries. We spent
some six weeks driving across the States, and I wondered what I was
doing there. I didn't have a rationale for being there; it wasn't where I
wanted to be. After our time in Guatemala I couldn't bear the prospect
of yet more time in an affluent society.

Of course there were practical advantages. It was a relief to
be able to drink the water, throw the paper in the loo. At last there
was good bread, unsugared fruit juice; we even found Marmite. On
the downside the expense was frightening – we began to run through
money at an alarming rate.

Naples, Florida, is the home of Leslie, an American writer
and former client, and his wife, Pat, who are dear friends, now in
their seventies. It was also my first experience of a particular type of
American town – green, spacious, sumptuous houses, but a town on
an inhuman scale, car-orientated, with no one walking and no feeling
of a local neighbourhood. I couldn't stand it. The heat was oppressive
– far more stifling than any we had encountered in Central or South
America. I felt claustrophobic, imprisoned, unable to go out without
a car. I was depressed at a vision of travelling through vast car-ridden
inhuman cities and endless noise – radio in the car, TV in the room,
Muzak everywhere else. Whither spirituality?

But then we arrived in Orlando, where Stephen had lived for
two years, and had been Clerk of the Quaker Meeting. It was more
intimate with pretty houses in neighbourhoods; less glamorous, much
more human. And, wonderfully, we were housed in the little cottage

next to the Meeting House. It was so good to settle for a week, cook for ourselves, make contact with all Stephen's old Quaker friends. And we received the two parcels I had sent on – full of presents to give and books to read. The cottage had a good presence: the atmosphere felt quite different, enabling. And Stephen and I were good with each other, on his territory. In this sometimes too secular leg of the journey, I felt spiritually advanced not only by the people we encountered and by the landscape, but by seminal books, placed, it would seem, in my way. From the Meeting House library, *Ordinary People as Monks and Mystics* by Marsha Sinetar spoke directly to me, was an affirmation of what I feel called to do, my need to express the reality of myself in my life. It's taken me a long time to get to this point, and I feel I need to get on with it.

Given Americans' preoccupation with the car, it was not surprising that much of this week in Orlando was taken up with acquiring one. At one point the difficulties seemed so unsurmountable that we looked at Greyhound buses, a much greener option, and more in touch with local people, but vastly more expensive. Trains ran rarely and did not cover the areas we wanted to see. We felt bulldozed into having a car. Renting for the six weeks would have been prohibitively expensive – $2,000 including insurance – so we were back to trying to buy and insure our own car. We finally acquired a ten-year-old Volvo, so immaculate that we were afraid to sit in it.

Stephen had wanted to show me all his favourite haunts but was frustrated by lack of time and the fact that so much had changed since he'd lived there. We did, however, visit Wekiwa State Park where we swam (with too many people) in the pure spring water, then canoed on the river. Stephen told me before we set off that there were alligators in the water. I knew he was joking: the Americans are paranoid about safety; indeed my complaint was always the extent to which they nannied us. The scenery was lovely – a cross, if that's possible, between the Charente in southwest France and the Amazon. Mirror-like water, lush vegetation, stark tree trunks lying in or sticking out of the water. I saw, for the first time, otters playing, myriads of turtles under the water, two blue-grey heron and other colourful birds that I could not name. But the boat was precarious and suddenly – did we hit a root? – we capsized. We were both in swimming costumes, the water was neither cold nor deep, but it was a terrible shock. Stephen swallowed a lot of water, and stood there choking, I was unable to speak for shaking. A wonderful young man jumped from a passing boat and helped to get our canoe onto the marshy muddy land, and I rescued our possessions which were floating around in the water. As we stumbled ashore, one of the rangers said, "Yes, of course there are alligators, but they wouldn't harm you." I had shared that water with alligators.

In the States, I wanted, perhaps naively, to get beneath the veneer, beneath the consumerism to the "real" America. Passing through at great speed, as we were, we were unlikely to make contact with poor communities except through the Quakers we encountered, but we did try hard to understand more of the Native American culture. On the surface, what we saw was deeply depressing. As we passed through Indian reservations, vast advertisements for casinos dominated the skyline. Native Americans have, it appears, captured the casino market. With their own laws and a measure of independence, they have found a way of making money by providing what is largely forbidden in the States – gambling centres. We also heard of the growing alcoholism in the reservations, the more dramatic since many Native Americans have a genetic intolerance to alcohol. Later, on a bus trip in Canada, we met a young Native American who was training to be an addiction counsellor in his own community: the problem was indeed a deeply rooted one.

Although our plan was to travel along the south of the United States, we diverted further north to visit the Cherokee communities of Oklahoma. We headed straight for the Cherokee Nation in Tahlequah, the headquarters of the second largest tribe in the States. Arriving early in the evening, we found the Cherokee National Museum closed, but were able to wander round the replica of an ancient village. Though it too was shut for the day, we met a young Cherokee man who was working there. We heard that a few years before he had had an accident at work which had damaged his back, an injury which had kept him off work for many months. Although he now had to work at a reduced level of activity, he said he had not received any compensation, and seemed surprised that I asked. He lived in the local reservation, and expressed contentment with his life, though I felt that was not the whole truth.

We visited the Museum the following day and informed ourselves of the terrible story of abuse represented by the Trail of Tears. The Cherokee, one of the five "civilised tribes", were pretty comfortable in 1830, when the Indian Removal Act came into force. They had their own form of representative government as well as a written language; many were affluent with extensive property, and some, we were astounded to hear, owned slaves. Because of divisions in the leadership of the tribe, they succumbed to the directive exiling them from their homes in Georgia, and moving them on to Oklahoma. During the terrible winter of 1838–39 some 4,000 Cherokee died in the thousand-mile march.

There is a considerable interest nowadays in Cherokee heritage from descendants even with one-sixteenth Cherokee blood – partly because there are material advantages for those who can prove their Cherokee descent. We learnt about what was available from the Nation offices. The social services were extensive, encompassing education, health, family assistance, help for business and training and employment services.

We talked to staff at the museum and in the nearby shop, but here and elsewhere we found it hard to penetrate the apparent absorption of Native Americans into the US mainstream. Yes, we were told, there were medicine men, but one would have to make an appointment some weeks ahead to meet them. Yes, it might be possible to stay with a Native American family, but nothing could be arranged at short notice.

We maintained an interest in Native Americans as we travelled and even got a list of Pow Wows round the country that we might be able to attend, but we were never in the right place at the right time. When we arrived in Santa Fe, we saw to our delight that the town had been taken over by a vast Native American craft fair. But what we found were besuited men sitting in front of extremely expensive pictures and artefacts, most of which seemed to have no identity separate from the rest of US culture. No reason why they should, but I was looking for more that was indigenous; seeking, without success, for a "real America" beneath the billboard consumerism.

In a way I found it in the travel itself, the only part of our journey that we spent in a car. We had planned a route through the South to Los Angeles, visiting Servas hosts, Quakers and friends along the way, and then up the West Coast into British Columbia. I say "we" but I'm afraid Stephen did all the driving. Although I had given up driving some 20 years before, I had reluctantly agreed to share it on this trip, but, mysteriously, for no doubt Freudian reasons, my international driving licence disappeared. (It was sent on to me later from wherever I had left it.)

Unlike trains and buses, there is no local life inside a car, except for the radio. Although we tussled about whether to have it on or off, we did light upon some programmes that enriched the texture of our trip. Especially the music on local stations: blues in Louisiana and Mississippi; country and western in Texas. Hearing the real thing in the real place is quite different, and we sang along with gusto. In fact we did have live experience of both. A close spiritual friend and her husband with whom we stayed in Baton Rouge, Louisiana, took us to a working men's blues club. We had been to New Orleans for the previous few days but this was of a quality I have rarely heard. Earthy, passionate playing and singing. And in Texas, derided Texas, we found ourselves in a motel next to a restaurant with a hillbilly band. It was enormous fun.

The other voices that stayed with me from the radio were those of the evangelical preachers. One in particular, whom we seemed to be able to get all over the country, was a minister from a cathedral in California, appealing unashamedly for funds.

"Numbers are down, get your registration in and get your ass down here. I've been appointed above you and have the right to tell you what to do."

But in general the activity was all outside our car windows. Driving mainly on the highways, rather than the impersonal interstates, we felt more in touch with humanity and signs of its existence, and with the environment as, at a slower speed, we could have the air conditioning off and the windows open. We settled in to a different kind of life from the earlier phases of our travels: long drives through magnificent scenery – vast forests, swampland in Louisiana and Mississippi, huge fields and some hills in Arkansas and Oklahoma. An experience of small-town America, amplified by Bill Bryson's *The Lost Continent* and our splendid guide book, *Road Trip USA*. We travelled on Route 66 for quite a lot of the way, enjoying the crazy little cafés and memorabilia, particularly the famous though vandalised Cadillac Ranch in Texas – ten brightly painted Cadillacs upended in a field.

The cheap motels we stayed in much of the time were impressive. They were generally undistinguished buildings at the rough end of town – "You don't want to go there" – but for about $30 a night, we got a clean big room with bathroom, towels, a TV and phone, and usually a pool: such a luxury in the stiflingly hot weather of the Southern States in August.

So much was different: the ease of life and the plenty. Rich soil, great rivers, and enormous space – not just in the vistas, but round the unfenced homes, and between the carriageways on the road. There were acres of land everywhere. And there was nobody walking. There was never anyone on the streets, no one to ask the way. Just cars. And huge stores. It was hard to find little shops, though we tried, and occasionally found stalls selling water melon or "muscadines" – large grape-like, round, succulent fruit.

Strange sights, such as whole homes being transported on the interstates, RVs (Recreational Vehicles – caravans) so huge they have to tow a car, as a large yacht does a dinghy. The hoardings were a source of pleasure: not only the famous one on Route 66: "Rattlesnakes exit here", but at the entrance to a church: "Don't worry, Moses was once

Cadillac Ranch

a basket case too." A wealth of information about local life was available from the organisations that participated in the national "Adopt a Highway" movement: a mile or so of highway kept litter-free at the expense of, for instance, the local boy scouts or, in one case, the Wiccans. Much to Stephen's amusement, I rather fell for American trucks. The "rigs" were so handsome and beautifully maintained, with shiny chrome and big brightly coloured cabs – brilliant red, purple or blue.

But again the richness of the experience lay mainly with the people, "ordinary people" who chatted with us and helped us out: the diner waitress or motel manager, working long hours but keeping up a smile and going the extra mile to be helpful. And our Servas hosts, exemplifying the international friendship that the organisation stands for. Scotty in Little Rock, Arkansas, for example. We had been attracted by the description in the list of hosts of a lakeside home in the woods. As it turned out he and his wife had divorced since the list had been printed and Scotty's response to my call was: "I hope you're not calling about the quilting, because we're divorced."

Our stay was all that we had imagined. A Unitarian, Scotty shared a lot of our spiritual beliefs, and his way of life had been a dream of Stephen's for many years – tending trees, chopping wood. He also made wine and furniture in an outbuilding. It was a tough time for him; conscious of his new single state – with his house depleted of the shared-out furniture. We were the first people he had hosted on his own, and I think our stay was a pleasure for us all.

And then there was Lynne in Santa Fe, with a very serene home, close to town. She was a Sufi/Buddhist, Stephen's age, a hiker and an artist. Until she had hurt her back recently she had been a caving explorer. Small enough to go where others could not, she led the way down into previously unplumbed caves. Lynne's house had a little peace garden with a hammock, swinging chair and an outside "hot tub". As I sat on a bench, a hummingbird above my head, reading in the idyllic climate (85° Fahrenheit in the shade but very pleasant and cool at night), an impromptu Spanish harmonic singing group started up from a house near by.

With its unique round-edged adobe houses, Santa Fe is an attractive town, and a place where people walk. It is cultivated – and expensive. On a lovely hot night we went to the open-sided opera house to hear young professionals perform excerpts of a variety of operas – not light pops, but a demanding selection, sung by singers of real power and dramatic range. And on the bedside at Lynne's was another of those seminal books: *Women Who Bond* by China Galland. About the search for "fierce compassion", it spoke of the interface of faith and action, and women asserting the feminine – leaders acting out their faith. I was particularly inspired by the story of Sister Jessie, an Indian nun turned solitary, and I determined to track her down once we got to India.

We were hoping soon to get the chance to sleep out. We were to have four days between Santa Fe and Arizona, and Lynne gave us her spare sleeping bags – too heavy to backpack with, she had no use for them. As Stephen said, if we had stayed any longer she would have emptied the house for us. The night before we left, Lynne rescued a large black beetle from our room, and mentioned the pleasure of sleeping out and finding little footprints around her in the morning. I envied her her composure; I'm not good at creepy crawlies. Perhaps it is my challenge to become more at ease with the less obviously attractive of our fellow creatures, as she and others who live closer to nature do. Appropriately, in her peace garden is a statue of St Francis of Assisi.

We stuck to our resolution to sleep out and drove far into the pine forests to a basic campsite in Cibola National Forest reserve. It boasted pit toilets as its only facility, so we thought we would have a good chance of getting some peace and quiet. And indeed, that proved to be the case: there was only one other couple there. Jackie and her boyfriend were, it turned out, local people, a tough no-nonsense couple who camped there regularly, getting away from it all. They slept in their van, and were adamant that on no account were we to sleep out. The previous time they had come, they said, there had been bear prints all over the cab of their van in the morning. We had already been alerted, first by a double-page spread in the local paper that morning about a bear that had killed a 90-year-old woman in her home; then by a notice as we entered the site: "This is bear country". Our companions' warning was the final straw.

As a thunderstorm threatened, they insisted that we share their meal cooked over the open fire: a feast of steak, large-kernel corn stalks, and salad. They were hunters, going out from time to time to shoot elk and other animals for the pot, cutting them up and freezing them for consumption later in the year. They were unashamed about not stalking them on foot but driving to an appropriate spot and pointing the gun. But they were scathing about the trophy hunters who hunt animals only for their horns, and leave bleeding carcasses, wasted, on the ground. This was, in their eyes, sacrilege. If you kill an animal you owe it to that animal to make the most of its life: the traditional ethos too of Native Americans.

So we also slept in our car, but I lay awake all night, waiting for the sound of the bears.

As usual, the desert – my reason for wanting to be in this part

The Painted Desert

of the States – eluded us. Somehow we were never quite in the right place, trying to squeeze too much in and rushing from one place to another trying to find it. I woke one morning and unwisely blamed Stephen which precipitated another row and ruined our view of the spectacular red rocks of Sedona, awesome in size and colour. The previous day we had stopped spontaneously at the Painted Desert, which was so beautiful that it brought tears to the eyes of both of us – rolling red desert of different hues, "badlands" as they are called. If we had known, we would have camped down there. As it was, unprepared, all we could do was stand and stare.

Now that I had finished my store of Chinese herbs, menopause was back in force: a lot of hot flushes, emotional swings and lack of energy. And still the periods came. Cooped up in a car, in the confines of hotel bedrooms, bereft of my usual daily yoga practice, my joints were seizing up.

But, finally, in Arizona, we did sleep, if not in the true desert, then at least in scrub land miles from anywhere. It was an unforgettable night under a crescent moon and myriad stars. I was nervous about unknown animal life – we saw an owl fly over and heard a coyote call – so I did not sleep much. I am drawn with a fierce, almost irresistible longing to such deserted spots, and, though in practice my courage falters, the experiences remain powerfully central to my life.

After nearly a month in the States I reflected that it was almost stranger being in a country that speaks (nearly) the same language than a foreign one. Expectation is confounded more often, not just by different words (wash up/wash dishes) but how different things are. How hard it is to get oil and vinegar dressing, how milk for tea comes in a glass not a jug, how cars have no front number plates, how little fruit and few vegetables there are in cafés and diners in such a fertile land.

And, surprisingly, it was in the States that we had the greatest difficulty in accessing two of the most universal examples of modern technology: the internet and the telephone. When we arrived at Miami airport, in a hurry to hire a car until we could buy one, we simply could not get a telephone to work. To use the phone you needed a card; to get a card you needed change; to get change you needed to use a machine which simply would not receive our note. No shop would change it; we bought something we did not need to get change, bought the card, then found it was the wrong one for the particular machine. By this time it was growing dark and we were at screaming pitch with the machines and with each other.

And this problem was repeated throughout the six weeks we were in the States. In motel rooms, in machines on the street in the torrential summer rain, it was the wrong card, the card had run out, the phone simply would not take cards. In a country where we were moving on often every night, and needed to sort out the accommodation further down the line, it was a major preoccupation.

Email was my concession to contact with the outside world. I had not wanted to be in touch with people elsewhere; I wanted to be in the current country, mind, body and soul. But email gradually took me over: for arrangements further ahead; ensuring that the people we wanted to see would be available; dealing with paperwork such as the booking for the Trans-Siberian Express. It also meant we were in touch with our friends and relations back home, which was a heartwarming affirmation, but also a reminder of worlds I was trying to leave behind.

Everywhere we went, even in small towns in far-flung places, we ensconced ourselves in the local internet café for half an hour or so and caught up. But in the States, where computers are so widely found in people's homes, there were barely any internet cafés to be found. We did find, both in the USA and Canada, that we could usually use them in a local library.

As we turned north at Los Angeles, the air suddenly became cool – a wonderful relief after the intense heat. But all the magnificent scenery was out there, and I was still, after five weeks, in a car. As we wended our way up the dramatic coastal route from Los Angeles through Big Sur, my need for tranquillity, camping in a local site by the river, swimming in the glorious sunshine was overridden by Stephen's wish to see Monterey and Cannery Row. The latter had been revamped and was, as I had imagined, a tourist trap. Monterey was a pleasant enough middle-class town with people walking around, but it was very hard to find a cheap restaurant or hotel. Access to the beach was cut off, with walkers and joggers purposefully using the bike and pedestrian way along the line of the coast, divided from the beach by a high wire fence. To emphasise their deprivation, the path was marked out with sand to simulate beach. There was access from the expensive Aquarium, where from the packaged zoo conditions, humans could exit to look out over the sea and the coastline. I felt low, compounded by the terrible back, knee and hip pain that had been hounding me for a couple of days. Unable to concentrate on anything, feeling disjointed and overruled. I knew that there would be no chance of any immersion in the natural world until after San Francisco.

On September 1st we were stuck in Labor Day weekend traffic. Hoping for wilderness, but nervous at the possible illegality of sleeping wild in this tourist area, all we could get into was the Redwoods Resort and campsite. The name summed it up. Lovely redwoods, but a resort, noisy, choc-a-bloc. We stayed in a cabin and wished we had had the courage of our convictions and slept down by the river where it was quiet and beautiful.

We did have two final nights in the wild before we left. The first time was in Oregon, in a lay-by beside a creek that we found in the dark. The heat was sticky in our arctic sleeping bags; our sleep punctuated by the honking of geese over the water. We were woken in the middle of the night by blue lights flashing in our lay-by; the police had turned up. It was a false alarm, as it turned out, for they had come to talk to another driver, but I felt vulnerable, naked in my sleeping bag, lying on the ground.

Our last night in the States was more peaceful. On the slopes of Mount Olympia, overlooking the Strait of Juan de Fuca that divides the States from Canada, was a campsite high up in the pine forests. Reassured by the metal bear-proof boxes supplied to store our food, we slept on the ground among trees so tall and thick that we could not see the stars. It rained in the night but I did not wake.

Respect the wide diversity among us in our lives and relationships. Refrain from making prejudiced judgments about the life journeys of others . . . Remember that each of us is unique, precious, a child of God.

Advices and queries, 22

Although evangelical Quakers predominate on the West Coast of the States, we had gone to some trouble to dig out unprogrammed Friends, who were usually isolated in small groups. At Santa Fe Meeting, we had met Jane and Bill, who were visitors from Riverside, California and had invited us to stay with them when we got there. When we arrived, they were about to go out, and generously left us with the run of their comfortable condominium and their balcony with cat, dog and turtle. Both artists, their work covered the walls. The next day Jane showed me her writing, and we talked of mysticism and animals, and particularly of crows, which have for Jane a particular fascination. At night she went for a jog – her way of finding solitude – but Bill had to stay in the car not too far away to make sure she was safe.

Jane and Bill in turn had rung Friends in Los Osos who also put us up for a night. They were a delightful elderly couple: she a retired schoolteacher, he an artist with few words but a mischievous sense of humour, much expressed in his art. Such generosity to strangers. They lived near a little bay, which we explored after supper. It was intimate, very pretty in the evening light, full of modest canoes upturned on the shore, light years away from the ostentatious craft we had seen elsewhere. And there was no need to lock them up.

We had also taken a diversion to meet Jeanne in Florence, Oregon. She is part of a worship group that meets twice a month, but the other three members were away. We shared a Meeting for Worship and lunch, before her spell of duty at a second-hand book stall at a charity fair. Earlier we had had a delightful random encounter with a fish buyer, sitting at his ease in the harbour as we walked down in the early morning, and ate our breakfast on the quay. He had lived there, man and mischievous boy, with a brief spell in the navy. He was a warm, storytelling man, comfortable in his life, with lots of free fish, his only sadness a wife who didn't like to travel. A rooted countryman with an enviable peace of mind.

After all these liberal Friends, it was more of a challenge to come upon George Fox University. Seeing a signpost bearing the name of the founder of Quakerism, we couldn't wait to see it the next morning, and found we were in time for one of the bi-weekly tours of the campus. We heard from our guide, an enthusiastic young woman for whom everything was "awesome", that, as in Quaker schools in the UK, only a minority of the students are Quakers. The facilities were excellent; the student/teacher ratio admirably low; but – frequent attendance at chapel compulsory. As we entered the large hall in a stream of students, we were aghast to see their IDs being scanned to give them their "spiritual formation credits". The service included a talk by one of the staff about integrity:

"Too many people here are having their IDs scanned, and then going out the side door. That is simply not acceptable . . . Now I know that some of you do not want to be here, and that's fine."

This address was followed by the singing of catchy rock numbers, some singing along with enthusiasm, punching the air, others mumbling the words. A young man on the campus later confirmed that you could get exemption from attendance.

"What for?"

"Clash of schedule."

"Not clash of faith?"

"No."

———

Some years ago Alistair Cooke said that he had never managed to find "the real America"; perhaps it was naïve to imagine that we could. When he asked where it was, people would wave their arm and vaguely indicate that he should keep going west – well, we had gone as far west as it was possible to go.

Perhaps Steinbeck got it right. The humour, the irony, the warmth of affection with which he describes Cannery Row and its community make them glow. Doc, the character based on the founder of the Aquarium in Monterey, speaks for a real America when he talks of walking through several states *"because he loved true things . . . because he wanted to see the country, smell the ground and look at grass and birds and trees, to savor the country"*. He also spoke for us and the purpose of our visit to the States, however little we achieved it.

CHAPTER 6

Home from Home

"Friendship is an equality made of harmony," said the Pythagoreans. Friend-ship has something universal about it. It consists of loving a human being as we should like to be able to love each soul in particular of all those who go to make up the human race.

Simone Weil

British Columbia is beautiful, with some of the friendliest people in the world. Vancouver Island, in particular, is like a cleaned-up England, with pure air, clean streets, a pro-British culture and lovely landscapes reminiscent of Kent or Devon. In a strange way it conforms to the view of England that many people abroad have. Wherever we went, people talked of tea and cricket on village greens. All of which exists, of course, but has nothing to do with the London that we inhabit. When asked about English customs, our habitual response was that there are no widespread habits any more; everywhere is different – there is freedom and variety. We would describe with enthusiasm the richness of life in London: the cultural diversity, the arts, the lively social scene. As an English Quaker who lectures in contemporary British culture in St Petersburg said, the view the Russians have of England is of a nineteenth-century pastoral idyll. In a sense that is what we found in Canada and New Zealand, and is what attracts the English there in droves.

In northern British Columbia I wrote:

Strange how Canada does not affect me. I have never been attracted to it and my response now that I am here is much the same. It's pretty but not affecting. When we walk in the woods, as today, they are gracious, spacious, but dead, silent. Not a bird sings. We saw a squirrel and bear droppings but no other sign. And there is no view, save trees on every side.

But we were there for good reasons, even if not my own. Stephen's wish to visit his relations and revisit the places of his childhood in British Columbia was an important one, and one to be taken seriously. So I tried to make the most of being there and struggle to realise the spiritual content of everyday life. In general the morning (menopausal?) miseries at not living the life I wanted to lead dissolved into some degree of acceptance. My rewards were frequent significant encounters and a few powerful new connections.

Before we left England, I had mentioned my impending trip to a colleague at Quaker Social Action. She said: "Oh, you must meet my mother; she's involved in similar work to you, with Native Canadian women." I was thrilled to hear of a project that I might get involved with, and the possibility of getting to talk to Native Canadians, and contacted Susan, who wrote back with typical generosity: "I would love you to help with my project. Come and stay."

Susan and John live in a fine wooden house in the woods near Sidney on Vancouver Island. John does research on ice floes; Susan works in the community. By the time we arrived, though, some six months after our initial contact, her work had moved on, and she was no longer involved with Native Canadians on a day-to-day basis. She was, however, ready for a new challenge. When I talked about microcredit and its successful application in developed countries, she jumped at the idea and knew at once which groups in the community she wanted to involve: NGOs working with Native Canadians, former prostitutes, new immigrants and single parents. She and I roughed out a proposal overnight and took it to one of the groups locally, who greeted it with enthusiasm. I wasn't around long enough to take the matter further but she has done so, and a few months later emailed me to tell me that they had a committee in place, and a funding application underway.

Stephen and I stayed for ten days and settled into an idyllic way of life. He was as happy as a sandboy in the beloved Vancouver Island of his childhood, gardening, discovering that he likes dogs after all and walking them every morning and – less pleasantly – trying to sell the car. We both unwound, I literally too after five weeks coiled up in the car, as we took long walks and were more physically active round the house and the pretty, if principally retirement, little town. I caught up with practicalities too, getting my hair cut, films developed, spending time in the library emailing. One evening, I spent a couple of hours helping Susan take lavender off its stalks to make bags. A peaceful and traditionally female occupation.

But the richness of our time there lay for me in the friendship we built up. Susan and I clicked straight away and were able to share confidences to a degree remarkable after such a short acquaintance. I felt supported to spend time with a woman so like me, to talk of menopause, relationships, aspirations: social, spiritual and personal. It made up for what I was missing from my friendships at home, made me feel more grounded. I felt sure that this was a friendship that would endure.

In Victoria we stayed with Stephen's relations. His aunt, Lisl, an Austrian dancer who had been rescued from Vienna by her English husband in the late 1930s, was a volunteer at a shop called Global Village, which sold goods from third-world countries. To our delight we found there the coffee from the Sandinistan farm in Omatepe, Nicaragua, where we had stayed. Such connections condensed the world; affirmed a form of globalisation that was beneficent. Outlets like Global Village are crucial for co-operatives and small business in third-world countries which depend on making a living in a market broader than their own poor community.

Lisl was also a volunteer at the splendid Royal British Columbia Museum. The Native Canadian section gave us more insight into Native North American culture than we had been able to glean from our contacts in the States. There was an audio-visual display of animals with voices over which gave me a greater understanding of animism; of their belief in the connection between man and the animal world, a belief that was growing strongly in me.

We then headed up the island to visit Courtney/Comox, to where Stephen had been evacuated as a child – the main reason for our being in Canada. We travelled on a slow pottering train. It was a lovely journey up the coast, with pine trees and the occasional glimpse of the water in between. Looking out of the back of the train at the receding tracks was reminiscent of my own childhood journeys, and as Stephen larked about in an empty carriage, one could well believe that the last time he had been here was when he was seven. We visited Norah, now 92, the woman who had brought him to British Columbia, and whom he had not seen since. We canoed on the sea at Kye Bay, where he had spent many happy holidays, and visited the grand house in the grounds of which he had lived, and which was now being restored.

It was on Vancouver Island that we said goodbye to our car. We had bought a mobile phone so that would-be purchasers could contact us, and after a number of newspaper advertisements, we finally sold it for what we had paid for it. Stephen was sad to hand it over and not happy at the prospect of being once again in backpacking mode. I was relieved at having sold the car and that we were handing it on in good order; also, predictably, glad to be without a car, back on the road.

There was one more important encounter before we left the country. We had decided to delay our flight to Hawaii in order to visit Stephen's cousin, Marion, who lives in some isolation with her husband Jim, in Houston, a community in the pine woods of northern British Columbia. It took us three days by boat and bus to get to this most northerly part of our journey so far, and we were, it turned out, the first of the family to go there. Marion and Stephen, who were evacuated together, had a great deal to talk about on family matters, and spent a good deal of time poring over photos.

I felt a strong affinity with this spiritual cousin, a Quaker in all but name. As I helped her prepare lunch at a local high school, Marion and I chatted about our shared love of spiritual books, and also about her own writing. It was also rather fun serving the children at lunchtime; Marion and an assistant worked at the speed of lightning, collecting in money and handing out pizzas, hot dogs, tacos and ice cream. Stephen and I also spent an evening with Jim, a pastor of the United Church, at his Bible class. The subject was the Beatitudes, a passage of the Bible to which I feel close, but sadly that evening was largely about organisational matters. I did admire Jim in his approach to property: "If I take in a hitchhiker, and he steals my camera from the back seat, I feel it is my fault for leaving it there," and I shared his abhorrence of churches that hold on to money. Inheriting a silver teaset, he had immediately given it away: "What would I need with a silver teaset?"

CHAPTER 7

The 9/11 Factor

Mankind has to get out of violence only through non-violence. Hatred can be overcome only by love. Counter-hatred only increases the surface as well as the depth of hatred.

Gandhi

*I*t was of course the year of September 11th.

In the six months before those attacks, we had ample proof of the preoccupation with America that is wrestled with by most of the rest of the world. In Rio, we got into conversation with an elderly man at the next table in a restaurant – he turned out to be a judge. After a little while he burst out: "Why do the British always hang on to the coat tails of the United States?" We could not answer; knew that it was all too true, particularly in the bombing of Iraq against which we had held a silent vigil in London some years before.

One cannot travel through Central America without being aware of the overwhelming influence of the USA. The history of involvement with corrupt regimes is too recent, too fresh. And in many places the local currency is disregarded in favour of the mighty US dollar.

In the steamy colonial town of Leon, Nicaragua, we came across a Sandinista rally, full of young people dancing on the stage, but also attended by the old faithful, one of whom asked me,

"What do you think of America?"

It was impossible to answer. I think all sorts of things about America.

But when pressed, I said, "I think America is good at democracy in its own country, not so good at it in other countries."

A simplistic response, but one which went down well.

And in the capital, Managua, where we stayed at a Quaker guest house one Saturday night, hoping to find a Meeting for Worship the following morning, we had come across a group of American students who knew nothing of Quakerism. When Stephen asked the leader of the group if he was a Quaker, he replied, "No, I am an American"!

In Honduras we met a young American teaching history. I could not imagine what kind of history an American might be teaching in Honduras . . .

We were in the United States itself, in August. One of the reasons for wanting to drive right across the States was to get a feel for the whole country, for the hugeness of it, and for a sense of middle America. Like many English people, I have friends in New York and on the West Coast, hardly typical of the Republican majority. I wanted to understand where it was that their foreign policy came from. During those five weeks, driving mainly on the highways, and avoiding the impersonal over-landscaped interstates, we certainly had a real taste of that enormous, varied and beautiful country, and its intensely friendly people. People in the car park, the shopping mall, at the motel, everyone took an interest. Seeing our Florida plates, they asked us about Florida, then hearing that we were from further afield, they were fascinated by our travels, immensely helpful – all over, in Oklahoma, in New Mexico, in Arizona, in Texas. And in the deep South.

In Mobile, Alabama, described as a New Orleans without the tourists, we came across our first real Republicans – Daughters of the American Revolution: two delightful elderly southern belles, immaculately dressed and powdered, running an old colonial house as a museum. Finding that we were English, the one showing us round dimpled with pleasure, somewhat embarrassingly deferring to what she assumed was our greater understanding of what is old, and served us with tea in bone china and home made cookies. She said she had been to London and loved it. Having sensed her racist tendencies, I said mischievously that I loved its cultural diversity and richness.

"Oh, yes, I saw so many Japanese."

I was thinking of Afro-Caribbeans, Bangladeshis, Indians, dozens of ethnic residents; she was obviously thinking of the tourists.

"Oh, you must have stayed in Kensington."

"Yes, how did you know?"

Everywhere we went intense patriotism was in evidence: many porches boasted a US flag; some, the flyer "Proud to be American". Fine, but how do they feel about those who are not?

In Arizona, desperate for some wilderness, we decided to spend a night under the stars. We drove down a dirt track in the midst of scrub desert, our main fear being that the owner might turn up in the middle of the night with a shotgun. He did arrive, but early in the evening, before we had bedded down for the night. With a horse box, not a shotgun, he stopped to pass the time of day. When he heard we were English, he was delighted and said:

"Oh, I'm English. My mother's Scots and my father's Welsh. That makes me English, doesn't it?" Shaking us by the hand, he drove off the 20 further miles across his land to his home.

Kindly people, and easy to make fun of, but with a frightening ignorance of the rest of the world and what is being done in their name. There are no national newspapers in the States – the *New York Times* and the *Washington Post* not being representative of the parochial press in most provincial towns, which do not have foreign correspondents and rely on government-biased agency reports for their news. And the vast majority of Americans do not travel, have never left their own country. Without that education, that contact with others, how are we to understand people of different countries and faiths?

On September 11th itself we were just over the border in British Columbia, Canada. Woken by early phone calls in the wooded house in which we were staying, I stumbled out of bed to those stupefying images on the television in the study. After hours of sitting with our hosts, transfixed and in shock, Stephen and I walked up on to the local hill overlooking the harbour, and sat on a rock, feeling numb.

A few days later I wrote in my journal:

I tried to explain to [some friends] and to myself the numbness I feel about the American attack. Partly we are away from home and on the move; I do not see or hear much detailed news, but partly this feels like a climax of a confrontation that has thus far been below the surface. A confrontation

*between the foreign policy of the USA and its recipients; the distance
between the goals of other nations and other faiths and the possibility
of its achievement. I feel as if the world is in suspension, awaiting the
outcome. But what outcome can there be except further bloodiness. We
can only pray for peace and spread peaceful thoughts among others.*

The opportunity to do so came very soon afterwards. When we left
British Columbia to visit Stephen's cousin Marion, we took a ferry for
15 hours up the Inland Passage from Port Hardy to Prince Rupert – with
the reputation of being one of the most beautiful of all sea passages. In
the event the much-heralded trip was marred by ill temper and – after
two weeks of sunshine – the descent of cloud and rain. A terrible
disappointment except for the glorious sight – my first – of frolicking
humpback whales, flipping their tails and blowing.

On the boat I got into conversation with a thin-lipped woman
from Minneapolis, desperately upset at the events of September 11th.
She had not wanted to leave her country, but her daughter had paid
for her ticket and she didn't want to let her down.

With tears in her eyes, she said: "The Bible tells us there will be
war."

I tried gently to remind her about forgiving our enemies,
said that we should pray for peace, try to show a better way. I was
aware that I was spouting platitudes, but was trying to meet her on
her own ground, where I might be understood. She was a Lutheran
and worked with Ghanaian refugees, but veered uncomfortably from
the charitable to the punitive, sure that the military option was not
only inevitable but right in the eyes of the Lord. It was a surprisingly
moving encounter and we parted with seriousness and sadness. I was
grateful to have met someone whose views, if reported to me, would
have seemed another reinforcement of a stereotype.

Ten days later, on our way out of British Columbia, Stephen
stopped to buy a newspaper in Prince George. There was none to
be had. The newsagent had received nothing since before September
11th. The only papers on the racks, ironically, were old copies
of *Newsweek*, with a cover story voicing the kind of criticism of

President Bush that was by now an unpatriotic impossibility. In Vancouver, on a bus from the airport into the city for the few hours that we had there, a Macedonian woman told us very forcibly that she did not like the English, a salutary reminder of attitudes that we prefer not to hear. If we align ourselves with the Americans we will draw to ourselves the same kind of unpopularity abroad as they have experienced for years.

As we made our way round the world the events of that day reverberated in many encounters. We went back into the USA when we arrived in Hawaii on September 22nd. I was struck by the diverse population, with *haulis* (whites) very much in the minority, and many Chinese and Japanese as well as Polynesian. Although the US flag was very much in evidence, there was too quite an anti-white sentiment. We stayed in the Quaker Meeting House, and with a few members of the Meeting, attended a forum about September 11th organised by an East/West society at the university. The panel was high-powered and largely hawkish, chaired by a Supreme Court judge; the audience, spilling out into adjoining rooms with many of us standing in the doorways, fired at them a reassuringly critical battery of questions. The bombing of Afghanistan had not yet started but was evidently on the cards. The resistance to any such possibility among the varied audience – students and local residents alike – was cheering.

———

By the time we reached Auckland, New Zealand, the bombing, supported by the British, was well underway. We joined a group of Quakers in a large demonstration. As the procession made its way through the city, we stopped, to my shame, not only outside the US Consulate, but the British one too. It was the first time I had been in a demonstration abroad which had in its critical sights my own country. I felt deeply upset: torn between a sense of belonging and a sense of shame. I tried to hand a note in to the British Consulate but was told by one of the policemen that everyone was out of town.

In Canada we had been in the privileged position of being able to access news both from Canada and from the States. The US, of course, was the country under attack: not surprising, really, that its news coverage was, for a while, utterly vengeful, whereas the Canadians from the beginning were asking "Why?" "Why are the Americans so disliked?" It wasn't until we saw a copy of the *New York Times* a little later that we realised that there were voices in America, however much in the minority, that were asking questions too. Everywhere we went from then on, those questions were being asked. Only in Tonga, where we first heard of the bombing of Afghanistan, were there voices of support.

In Thailand we were reminded of a chilling American export that has been a powerfully evil influence in the world: the training given to Latin American soldiers by the notorious US Army School of Americas, based in Fort Benning, Georgia. Our friend, Karol, told us the story of a South American woman who had been abused and tortured by soldiers trained at the "school". She had brought her story to the attention of the press in the States and lobbied government, but to no avail. No one wanted to listen. I have since heard that the US has changed the name of this "school". Not surprisingly.

In India the ramifications of September 11th could be felt in the intensification of ongoing tensions between Hindus and Muslims, notably over the demolition of a mosque and the subsequent plans to build a temple on the site of Lord Rama's birthplace. When the Parliament Building in Delhi was attacked on December 11th, links with the attacks in America were made, as they were, of course, when the American Center in Kolkata was attacked – on the day we arrived there. This was the only occasion on which we felt drawn in. The project in Orissa that we were due to visit suffered some disruption in the usually harmonious relations between the Hindu and Muslim staff, and we were asked to delay our visit.

Otherwise, as in the States, we felt strangely removed. On December 23rd I wrote:

Strangely, altho very aware of world events, and the tensions in India itself,

*we don't feel drawn in. It's a bit like visiting in Ireland when everyone outside
is reading about bombings in the North. Life goes on as normal for most
people. Perhaps we are able to achieve some balance and distance; perhaps we
are numbed by distance from home and the practicalities of moving around.*

When we left India in March, people asked, "Isn't it dangerous? I'm
surprised you went." Such is the distance between external views and
how it feels on the ground away from the actual trouble spots. After we
left, the risk of war became greater, but I imagine that lives went on as
usual in most parts of that vast country. On the day it was announced
that British residents and visitors were being asked to leave India and
Pakistan, my photos of India arrived. As I looked through pictures of
that richly varied and beautiful landscape and the smiling faces of its
inhabitants, I prayed that the leaders would draw back from the brink.

It was a strange year in which to travel: a time in which the
relations between one country and another, and particularly between
those in the developed world and those which are developing, were
more acutely focused. I had not wanted to spend time in developed
countries, but, on looking back, I can see that it was valuable to
experience views from different countries and to carry messages from
one to another. We are one world, and we all have responsibilities
towards each other.

CHAPTER 8
The Simple Life

Live simply that others may simply live
                        Gandhi

The really abundant life is not to be found in the clutter of material complexity but in simplicity

                    L. Hugh Doncaster, in *Quaker Faith and Practice*

On our flight from Hawaii to Tonga, we crossed both the Equator and the date line, so a day was crossed out of our diaries. It was an appropriate demarcation, for our three weeks in Tonga were quite unlike our time in the countries before and after it: an oasis between chunks of first-world travel. For once it was an experience – in this case of a South Sea island – that conformed to the image. It was Paradise. As we looked down from the plane to the first of the islands, tears came to my eyes at the sheer beauty of the atolls: turquoise strips, ovals, circles in a blue sea.

The Kingdom of Tonga comprises 171 islands, of which 40 are inhabited, spread over an area of nearly 700 square kilometres. Though his country is a constitutional monarchy based on the British system of parliamentary democracy, the King is one of the most powerful monarchs in the world. He appoints the cabinet ministers for life and, of the 42 parliamentary representatives, only nine are elected by commoners. The power of the monarchy and ruling class is matched by a veneration for religion which has played a major part in the development of the country from the Wesleyan missionaries in the early nineteenth century to the more recent inroads of the Methodists and Mormons.

The strength of the monarchy and the churches mean that, despite a wish to bring the country into the modern economic world, there is an equal wish to keep traditional customs and values. Although its foreign affairs came under British protection from 1893 until 1970, Tonga is the only country in the region not to have been colonised by a European power, which is perhaps why it has had relatively few tourists and has kept its identity.

When we landed, it was raining, and the capital, Nuku'alofa, was somewhat of a disappointment. Our first impression was of many young people on the streets, macho in a rather unfriendly way. We had been told how friendly Tongans were, but in fact that was not the case: they are a dignified, reserved, somewhat impassive people, though apparently they are more guarded in front of superiors or foreigners. Tongan men and women are large and statuesque, the men wearing skirts called *tupenu*, both sexes wearing *ta'ovala*, fraying woven mats or fronds round their waists, as a sign of respect – the older the mat, the more prestigious it is.

On the main island, Tongatapu, we stayed at Toni's guest house, long renowned among backpackers and a mine of information. Toni was the name of the lugubrious, knowledgeable and sexist Lancastrian – sixtyish with a long grey ponytail – who owned the guest house. It was also the name of the precocious five-year-old son of the Tongan couple who looked after the place. Young Toni spent all his time with his namesake and spoke fluent English, unlike his father. To the confusion of outsiders, he called both men "Dad".

We went to a Tongan feast, attended not only by tourists but by Tongans as well, including a local couple who owned an office equipment shop in the town. He was Tongan, she Fijian, and it became clear, on talking to her alone, that she thought Tongans were distinctly inferior – she as a Fijian was much more sophisticated.

Toni's tours of the island are famous. The lovely empty roads were lined with palm trees, caro and squash on either side, small box bungalows, people in their Sunday best. Most of all, in one spot, vivid turquoise parrot fish seen from a cliff, down in the clear blue and turquoise depths; a long-tailed tropic bird – elegant streamlined white, then a kingfisher in blue and white. We also had the extraordinary experience of swimming in a cave in the dark. Holding our torches, we undressed on the steep rocks beside the freshwater pool then, turning off the torches, we gingerly lowered ourselves into the water. I was one of the last in and did not venture far, fearful of scraping myself on the edge of an unseen rock.

———

We had to give up the idea of sailing. Chartering was prohibitively expensive and opportunities for crewing unlikely unless we wanted to sail to New Zealand. So we decided to head for tranquillity instead. Of the groups of islands near by, Ha'apai was recommended as the quietest and, of that group, 'Uiha looked the most attractive. I had been adamant that I wanted to travel there by ferry, not fly to Pangai, the capital of Ha'apai. Everybody said I was mad and gave graphic descriptions of how terrible the ferry was, how rough the sea, how the decks were awash with vomit. Very reluctantly, finding that the ferry on the day we could go was even slower and more uncomfortable than the others, I gave in to the universal pressure, only to find that the ferry had in any case been cancelled because of strong winds!

The eight-seater plane to Pangai felt hairy enough, though my fears were dissipated by the obvious competence of the young woman pilot. But it was nothing compared to the trip that followed it: an hour in a small motor boat over tumultuous seas. Despite the equal competence of Assa, our captain, I was not only exhilarated but terrified as the boat rode up the sides of massive dark blue waves. The boat was full of people, including our hostess Kanoli and assorted family, all of whom were quite relaxed. None spoke English. Why had our guide book said that one did not need to learn Tongan? There was only one lifebelt, and all insisted I wore it. I was resistant – why should I as a woman and a foreigner take precedence? – but eventually gave in.

The "resort" or hotel was made up of a compound on the beach containing four huts or *fales*. Behind it were the village hall, village phone and the "village green": a large patch of uneven grass, overrun with chickens, dogs and pigs. Both here and in South America I took a quite different view of pigs. Unlike those in England, those here were small and brown, running wild: attractive self-possessed little animals. The main activity on the green was tennis, played every afternoon by the young men of the village, with whoops and laughter. It took a week before they asked if I would like to play, which I did, in a long skirt. I felt I'd been accepted.

Our *fale* was simply lovely, with matting on the floor, and the walls and ceiling covered in strongly patterned *tapa*, the beaten bark of candlenut and mangrove, which all the women made locally. A shower room and lavatory were in separate grass huts outside. Torches, as usual, were essential.

After our first meal of delicious unicorn fish and breadfruit chips, we realised that we would have to cook for ourselves – the dinners were simply too expensive. But it was easier said than done. Everyone grew their own fresh food and the two local shops, open only on request, stocked very few items, such as tinned corned beef, condensed milk and toilet paper. It was hard to scrape together enough food to make a decent meal, and we ate rather repetitively while we were there.

There were some two hundred people in our village, Felemea, rather more in the village at the other end of the island. For a while we were the only visitors on 'Uiha, though a few others came and went. The indigenous way of life was mostly money-free – ours seemed the only money to change hands. The islanders lived off the fish they caught and the fruit and vegetables they grew in little plots in the interior of the island. Our hostess Kanoli was having a difficult time. Since her husband was ill and recuperating on another island, she had to look after her daughter, handle the resort and go to her smallholding to tend the crops. But it was very much a family affair, with her brother-in-law, Assa, taking charge of the fishing, the boat and ferrying of passengers from Pangai. In Tonga all is shared within the extended family. There's no real sense of possession even of children who are essentially brought up by the broader family.

The weather at the outset was disappointing: strong winds and rather chilly. On our first morning, we went for a beachcombing walk in the rain along the beach to the tip of the island. Not a person was to be seen for several hours, just a couple of birds, molluscs in their shells, and one set of dog tracks. Fine, pale sand, tranquil turquoise and blue sea – the stuff that dreams are made on. And beyond was the roar of the ocean at the edge of the reef. There was harmony between us and in the world around as we walked, paddled, talked of theology and shells. On our return, Kanoli presented us with some delicious chocolate cake, made for her daughter's school.

That evening we were joined by a Danish couple who, with Stephen, did a dance on the beach to bring out the sun, while I swam in the rain, laughing at the sight. And, lo and behold, the sun appeared in a glorious sunset before we retired for the night. I read *Mutiny on the Bounty* while I was there, enjoying the descriptions of islands close to ours. The mutiny itself happened off the nearby island of Tofua and the crew had landed for a while, but the islanders drove them off, killing a seaman in the struggle.

One morning we were awakened at 4 a.m. by the strong beat of a drum. Stephen shot out of bed to see what was up. When I heard the tolling of the village bell, I too got up, sure that there must be a shipwreck or similar emergency. It turned out to be a call to prayer. Drawn by the sound of stentorian singing, I tentatively entered the back of the nearest church to find, sitting in lamplight, one elderly man, one young woman and two elderly women in hats, generating harmony of a power such as twenty might create. They were singing with their entire bodies – a raw, magnificent sound. When the generator provided electric light, I saw to my horror that, apart from being unwashed and without underwear, my jumper, donned in the dark, was inside out, and everyone else was in their best clothes.

We developed quite a routine. A torch and a bottle of rainwater on either side of our saggy bed each night, the lighting of the hurricane lamp. Stephen rising early for his morning run along the beach, little boys, running with pigs, laughing at him. We then watched Assa disentangle the night's catch from the nets: a pailful of spotted, striped and orange fish. Making breakfast, then taking a packed lunch of crackers, processed cheese and a tomato. Cold showers, the ubiquity of sand and I, almost permanently barefoot, rinsing the sand off my feet in the tap before entering our *fale*.

Once the sun came out, we were in our element. One day we asked Assa to drop us off on a neighbouring uninhabited island – reputed to have the most beautiful beach in Tonga (the world?) and good for snorkelling. Stephen snorkelled and I later went out with the mask over my eyes – I felt claustrophobic with the mask over my nose – and saw, for the first time in my life, a coral reef. I was so overwhelmed by the tranquillity and beauty of it, the coral itself and the myriad brightly coloured fish, that I came ashore and just sat on the beach and wept. The sun was scorching. The flaws in our Paradise were flies, vast black sea slugs, swift-moving big black crabs that looked like tarantulas and bumped into me as I sat on the beach, and the fear of stone fish and eels, both pretty vicious. I wasn't too keen on starfish close to, either: the plump and fleshy black one I saw in the shallows was very different from my idealised image.

'Uiha sees very few tourists. For that reason it was quite hard to penetrate the lives of local people. They kept themselves to themselves, apart from the children, who accosted us as we walked from our village to the other, past the school that serves both. There were hordes of children in smart blue uniforms on foot or on bike, playing marbles, trying out their English on us, alternately sweet and tiresome. We had several other encounters on the walk, particularly with the town officer, who was mayor and policeman in one, a stocky confident man who offered us the use of his boat; and with a young woman gathering palm fronds for a fire, who offered me food. Earlier in the day, as I walked on the beach alone, I had met a large bare-chested man carrying a machete. Unsure whether his intentions were friendly or otherwise (given the reported attitude of men here to women on their own) I turned back.

The village hall was the venue for a couple of important events while we were there. I sat in on one, held by a couple of young women lawyers (there are eight women lawyers in the whole of Tonga) from the main island. They had been given a UNESCO grant to conduct surveys throughout Tonga on the subjects of domestic violence, sexual abuse and land law. I talked afterwards to the young lawyers, who ate at our resort: a new generation of Tongan women, leading the way to emancipation.

The other event was a workshop on electricity, which was to be introduced on the island the following year. It was to be co-operatively owned, as was the water. One of the woman facilitators came into our compound and flopped down on the ground, recovering from her journey and the heat. A big handsome woman in middle age, Mele was an interpreter for the New Zealand speaker who had come over for the workshop.

It was an extraordinary encounter. She was eager to hear of our fellowship in Quaker Meetings, warmed immediately to the idea of group silent worship. In an over-busy life as head of the Sunday school in her Methodist church, with a full-time job and six children aged 4 to 16, she found a lack of communion with God. She told me she had recently skipped an afternoon church session to spend time alone with her Bible, and was surprised to hear that we were more interested in the spirit from which the Bible comes than in the Bible itself. Also, that we believe in a direct unmediated relationship with God. She understood intuitively, asked the subjects of my "meditation" today, "as we will probably not meet again". When we parted, after just half an hour together, she said, "I will never forget you." Nor I her.

I had fewer hot flushes at this time: there was no stress and few rows. I was getting fitter again, and I was singing, always a measure of my morale. Some local children loomed up on the beach one night when Stephen and I were lying in hammocks looking at the stars. They laughed and poked at us, but then they asked for an English song. We asked for a Tongan one, which was lovely, then got them singing an English round. Stephen noticed one child who could not speak, so to involve him we taught them Hokey Cokey, which was a great success. Inevitably after that we were approached at all hours of the day, and asked for Hokey Cokey.

Tonga has a traditional culture with strict codes of behaviour, and it is a surprisingly sexist one. No woman may inherit or register land. There are constraints on how women dress (no shoulders or

arms showing) and if bathing, we are expected, as in Muslim countries, to do so fully clothed. I swam in my costume out of sight of the
village, so as not to offend local sensibilities. Men can be fined for not
wearing a shirt. The women's dancing is static with decorously gentle
and submissive arm movements and gestures of the head. The men's,
however, is dynamic, strong and sexy – they have good solid, fit-look-
ing bodies.

It would seem that this prudishness stems from the missionaries.
Religious observance is certainly important, with no tour guiding,
work or swimming allowed on a Sunday. In our village there were
four churches: Tongan, Congregational, Baptist and Mormon. It was
hard to spot the Mormon church; to begin with we had mistaken the
tidy, fenced-off compound with its forbidding-looking building for a
prison. Many of the people we met were Mormons, including Kanoli,
who told us that during her training she had been sent to the States on
secondment, and had not been allowed to contact home. A Mormon
taxi driver in the capital told us that his faith taught him to listen to
his wife and spend time with his four daughters, but he still wanted a
son! We suggested to our host, a grave and hard-working man, that
it would be good to have an evening together to talk about their faith,
thinking we would be able to share a little about Quakerism too. Sadly,
Assa couldn't find the time, but, as we left, he asked for our names and
address, so that he could ask one of his Mormon brothers in the UK to
come and visit us. Not what we had in mind!

Although I knew that the catch was a mainstay of the island's
diet, I found it distressing most mornings to see a number of fish still
alive, flailing in the nets, drowning in the air. Distressing too to witness
the fear of a pig in a sack, taken one day on our boat trip to Pangai,
and another, squealing desperately, tied up and trundled along in a
wheelbarrow. And one night we decided to treat ourselves to dinner
cooked by Kanoli, and she presented us with the largest lobster I had
ever seen. Such a magnificent beast and such a cruel death. I had given
up eating lobster some years before, but found it difficult to refuse. Why
was I not a vegetarian?

One day I found a crawling shell in our *fale*. I had never seen shells living and moving till Tonga, never felt the immense richness of living beings till now. Reading a chapter on "God in the World" in *The Perennial Philosophy* was wonderfully apposite and thought-enriching as a confirmation of all we saw about us – the beauty of the sea, a palm tree, a shiny black patterned cowrie, a coconut fallen from the tree. A God of the fullness as well as the heights, all inclusivity.

CHAPTER 9

Among Friends

I do not think that I am alone in my certainty that it's in my relationships with people that the deepest religious truths are most vividly disclosed.

George Gorman, in *Quaker Faith and Practice*

While we were away, the worst of the foot and mouth epidemic was raging in England. Other countries were at pains to protect themselves, and on arrival at Auckland airport, New Zealand, our boots were taken away and washed. I had not had any intention of going to New Zealand, but it was on our route from Tonga, and in the event I was overwhelmed by the friendliness and calm efficiency of the people we met. After Customs there was a free phone, free tea and coffee, excellent information services, an ATM and, right outside, an airport bus that took us to the doorstep of our destination with courtesy and despatch. When we came back to the airport a week later for our flight to Australia, we discovered that it had left three days before – we had forgotten to update our schedule. The airline staff not only did not charge us for the change, but put us on a specially expedited entry at our next stop. Astonishing.

While in Auckland we stayed next to the Quaker Meeting House, in a guest house run by highly professional wardens. Alan and John were actually the wardens of Melbourne Meeting House in Australia, but they had done a swap for a couple of weeks. Both of them had English connections. John, a quiet gentle man and an artist of distinction, was from East London, and bore an uncanny resemblance to an uncle of Stephen's from the same area. Alan, who is a New Zealander and was back on his own turf, had run a stall at Camden Lock, near our own flat in North London. They were friendly and generous while maintaining their necessary privacy and distance.

Auckland was the one place in which our talk "Are Quakers

Christians, Mystics or Social Activists?" did not go down well. It was a sophisticated audience, and we felt we were telling them nothing new. Unlike British Quakers, who examine themselves painfully on the subject, they did not feel that the question of the Christianity or otherwise of Friends was an issue, and, as for social action, we felt we were teaching our grandmothers to suck eggs.

Friends took us in hand while we were there, and we met Clare and Linley, sisters deeply involved in Quaker work. Linley was Clerk of the Asia-Pacific section of a Friends' committee, and was an invaluable source of information as we travelled round "her" region.

There was little chance to explore in our one week in New Zealand, but we did spend a few days in the Coromandel Peninsula, travelling by bus. We stayed one night with Quakers in a house on the edge of a nature reserve near the town of Thames. Philip and Phoebe are off the grid, existing on solar energy, a model of simple living. After a slow start, we had a lively discussion, especially about homelessness, and it turned out that they had helped process books for our mobile library when they visited London. We had met before!

In the morning, there was a lovely dawn chorus. We had been starved of birdsong and, in a land without indigenous predatory mammals, there are a lot of birds. Phoebe is involved in the preservation of indigenous species of flora and fauna, and resistant to foreign ones. But there was a wide variety of both as we walked in their extensive grounds and into the bush. We crossed a swing bridge; a "sway" or "hammock" bridge might be more appropriate – definitely not for the faint of heart; and in the evening I went for a second, more substantial, "tramp".

Our visit to Christine, a Servas host and resource teacher, was most timely. She had read advertisements for Quakers in the paper and had thought of writing off for information. As we swam in a hot springs pool, I answered her questions, and found her heart open to all that Quakerism stands for. On our last night, the three of us sat on the beach, wrapped up against the cold and eating fish and chips, with the stars bright overhead and the sound of the waves barely visible a few yards in front of us.

It was mid-October and the halfway point in our journey. After six months, many of my clothes were darned, and a dress, a pair of trousers and a swimming costume had been discarded and replaced. Medically we were pretty sound: I had had one spell of diarrhoea, in Bolivia, and now had a broken crown on a tooth; Stephen had had a chest infection in Peru and now was on antibiotics again, this time for a streptococcal infection (horrid yellow eruptions on his head, eye and foot). Stephen confessed that he was tired of moving on; I was still excited and keen, missing my kids and friends, but not homesick for any place, work or routine. If Stephen and I had been getting on better, I would not have felt so alone.

———

In Australia our time was thoroughly organised by local Friends, who had emailed us in South America: "Would you be free to give talk on Friday 13th at 5.30?" Three months ahead we had no idea where we were likely to be. We were on another continent in a metaphorical as well as a literal sense. But once there we were enfolded in Quakerdom, and we felt at home. In Sydney, in any case a lovely city, we were rescued from a rather unfriendly Quaker guest house by the kindness of the former clerk, Cathy, and her English husband Barry. Canberra, denigrated by all we met, was lit up by the graciousness of Katherine who had stayed with us briefly in England and her lovely husband, Glynne, who sadly died a few days after our departure. In Melbourne we were looked after by James who had never met us before but was prepared to host us for a whole week. He worked for a community organisation that helped problem families, and asked if I would talk about microcredit at their AGM, which I did, not expecting an audience of a hundred or so. After our return they emailed me about the design of a feasibility study and in July 2003 started a pilot project with refugees of several nationalities.

Stephen and I gave our usual talk in several places, and also talked about our travels at Victoria regional summer camp. Stephen, speaking from his heart about his spiritual doubts, found the audience much in sympathy. Frances, a friend of one of the members of our own Meeting, and who had visited Westminster in the past, generously took us out in her car for a day and a picnic in the Dandenong hills. It was there that I discovered that wild birds do not have to be afraid of human beings. Never having been shot at or pursued, they came to us, perched near us, obviously unafraid. It was such a startling revelation that I felt out of time – as if I had been given a flash of the eternal, a glimpse of what might have been possible in a prelapsarian world. It was a realisation that was to be underscored later, in other landscapes.

———

I find it hard to describe the bits of Australia that we saw: so English in some ways; so different in others: the light, the foliage, the brilliance of the birds, the sparkling water in Sydney Harbour, and the physicality of the lifestyle. It always sounded boring when people described it before we went, but felt attractive and natural when we were there. I was quite childlike in my response to the birds – and others much amused. In Sydney's botanical gardens the proliferation of ibises, which I had never seen before. In Canberra the crimson rosellas – primary blue and red flashing through the air; and in Katherine's garden a king parrot, magnificent in its red head and green wings. The brilliance of their colour was the epitome of "exotic".

Where we went there was very little sense of poverty or crime, though both exist, and very little evidence of Aborigines. Quakers in Australia have the same struggles with government policies, particularly on the subject of asylum seekers, and in tagging along with Bush in his "war against terrorism". We went with some Friends in Canberra to an ecumenical forum on refugees, held in a "Uniting" church (they prefer the continuous present to the past participle). United the meeting certainly was in its open-heartedness to refugees, and its condemnation of the government's fortress mentality. I offered solidarity from a British perspective, saying that they were not alone in their struggle against bigotry. In Australia the appalling sinking of a refugee boat the previous month, drowning 350 people, including children, seemed to have moved the nation, and seemingly shifted public opinion a little (though as the election proved soon after we left, not enough). At the meeting there were calls for action, calls for the taking in, at the very least, of unaccompanied minors held in detention, reminders that as Australians they had a shameful history with their own indigenous people, and were now repeating it against foreigners in need.

We did not go into the interior where we might have found ourselves in a foreign land. I had set time aside to visit a friend whom I hoped to pin down in some other part of Australia – ready to fly out to see her – but we lost contact, and I never tracked her down. However we were also seriously considering a complete change in our plans that would have taken us across Australia and into the outback.

While we were in New Zealand we had been invited to go to an evening run by the Women's International League for Peace and Freedom (WILPF), whose guest speaker was to talk about East Timor and the work she was doing there. Anna was, off her own bat, making an attempt to help the beleaguered inhabitants of East Timor after the end of the civil war. Finding that one need was for water pumps, she had advertised for them, and tracked down so many that she had to ask the New Zealand navy to take them out. Her current search was for cattle. The retreating armies had burnt and destroyed everything in their path, so much of the livestock in East Timor had been destroyed. She was sending out a bull and several cows, and was looking for funding for it. All gave without hesitation, and Stephen and I, captivated by her independent spirit, asked if we might be of any help.

We discussed teaching English, and the possibility of microcredit. We worked out that by skipping the next stage of our journey – Thailand – and breaking into our time in India, we could spend perhaps 12 weeks there. We did a lot of research, emailing contacts – Quakers and others – in East Timor, and found that the overland journey to Darwin would actually cost us more than the flight from there to East Timor and the change to our existing flight plans – going via Bali to

India. Anna had been scathing about the bigger agencies, especially the UN, whose staff she said lived luxuriously and expensively and who operated bureaucratically, and we found a similar negative response from official channels that we approached. East Timor had, we were told, chosen Portuguese as its official language, so English was not wanted, and in any case the agencies were beginning to withdraw. We did, however, have a warm invitation from a junior minister in East Timor, who asked if we might teach at his daughter's school. This research took up a lot of time and emotional energy during our stay in Australia, but in the end we decided that we would not be able to go for long enough to make a real difference – the drawback of the kind of travel that we were doing. Easy to feel that we might go there for a longer time once we got back to England, but it's a very long way.

It was a reluctant decision, and we both felt upset about it. I wondered if we had succumbed to caution partly because, after nearly three months, we had got too used to first-world comfort. I had certainly been apprehensive about the idea of East Timor; felt we had less energy – was I getting tired of travel? With some of the most exciting places to come – India and Mongolia – I hoped not.

Stephen said as we left that our time in Australia had been like a course at Woodbrooke, the British Quaker study centre: a concentration of time with Quakers – perhaps that's right. It certainly accounts for the feeling that we were not in a foreign country. The time in Canada, New Zealand and Australia, loving though it was, didn't feel like being abroad.

Silence in Bangkok

There is nothing in the world that resembles God so much as silence

Meister Eckhart

*C*hiangmai was probably the most tourist-ridden town of our journey.

We had taken the train north from Bangkok in my perennial search for tranquillity, but had found a town full of bars and restaurants with English names – home from home with cheap beer – and young people who, a generation ago, would have been found on a Greek island. Though we did manage to find little stalls selling noodles and a workshop where a man painstakingly rewound armatures, such traditional sights were squeezed in among a myriad signs for guest houses, treks and tours. Even in the *wats* (temples) there was little tranquillity to be found; rarely any garden in which to sit. On one occasion after a tentative approach, in suitably modest garb, I was chased out of the grounds of one by an irate elderly monk, whether because I was a visitor or a woman I didn't gather. It didn't say much for his loving kindness. That night I read in the journal of a young woman who came to live in Thailand the comment by an Australian monk: "The connections you don't see are the deepest." Well, they felt pretty deep at that moment.

It was also the first time we had come across a dirty hotel: despite pretty teak rooms, the bedding was filthy, and the pillow under the slip unspeakable.

So, after a day or so, at odds with both the place and with Stephen, I was catapulted into action and took off on my own, heading for Wat Phra That Si Chom Thong, a Buddhist monastery I had read about which was a couple of hours away by bus. I had not booked;

I was unsure whether I would be accepted. I had read that the course in Vipassana meditation required visitors to attend for a minimum of ten days, and I could only stay for four. Thankfully, I was accepted without question.

———

I worshipped Him the oftenest that I could, keeping my mind in His holy Presence, and recalling it as often as I found it wandered from Him. I found no small pain in this exercise, and yet I continued it, notwithstanding all the difficulties that occurred, without troubling or disquieting myself when my mind had wandered involuntarily. I made this my business, as much all the day long as at the appointed times of prayer; for at all times, every hour, every minute, even in the height of my business, I drove away from my mind everything that was capable of interrupting my thought of GOD.

Brother Lawrence

So, another world, and peace and quiet at last. The *wat* boasts a gilded Burmese *chedi* (stupa) built in 1451 and a sixteenth-century Burmese-style *bot* (sanctuary) with lovely carved wooden eaves. The compound also contains a meditation hall, a dining area and dozens of little meditation huts, in one of which I was billeted. I had a sleeping mat on the floor, a fan, even a chair, plus my own bathroom. There were several Westerners in the *wat*, together with about forty nuns, in white, and as many monks, in orange robes, all with shaved heads. I was taken under the wing of Jodi, a Canadian lay woman who was based at the *wat* much of the year, shown where to go, and lent a timer for my meditation.

It was to make contact with a Buddhist culture that I had come to Thailand but these were some of the toughest few days of my life. Dressed in the white trousers and tunic of novice nuns, we were required to rise at 4 a.m., breakfast at 6, lunch at 11.30, and eat nothing further till the next day, though drinks were allowed. We were requested not to sleep during the day, not to read, write, make phone calls, listen to the radio or music, and to talk as little as possible. Certainly meals were in silence. There really was little that we could do except meditate, and it was in fact the case that any conversation I had did interfere with my attention during meditation.

The aim of the training was mindfulness: to live in the present, pay attention to what we were doing; in the words of Brother Lawrence, the seventeenth-century monk whose book I carried round the world, to follow "The Practice of the Presence of God" in all that we did. An active title for an active expression of our faith. The form it took in this temple was individual repetitive and timed meditation, walking or sitting slowly and mindfully, stopping to acknowledge any distraction such as an awareness of the senses or a movement of thought. Ten minutes walking; ten minutes sitting; then starting all over again. Gradually the sessions were built up until each was for half an hour and included some variations. Each morning we met alone with a supervisor, in my case a kindly but meticulous young Canadian man. Slow mindful activity, trying not to notice out of the corner of the eye the other white-clad wraiths moving slowly around the meditation hall. I often found it easier to do it in my room.

All the meditators acknowledged the toughness of what we were doing – the aching back, constant sleepiness, despair about achieving anything, the wish to run away. After hours of meditation, I found myself deeply resistant, pushing myself further, through a barrier, and sometimes into mystical awareness: an intensification of normal life. One morning, falling about with tiredness, I forced myself on, coming to a point when I cried and wanted to give up altogether. Forcing myself further, I found myself in a timeless place, breath quickened, gold covering all. This time I cried with gratitude, knew experientially what I have read about so often. I immediately began another round and the walking exercise was imbued with a new intensity. Then all faded and was as before. When I reported the experience the next morning, I was reminded of the importance of transience, that I must not hang on to it. Indeed, I had already returned to the humdrum and the fatigue.

The experience was painful not only because of frustration and the stamina, patience and humility that was demanded, but because I had done my knee in on a hired bike in Chiangmai and was finding kneeling or sitting cross-legged – the required postures – well nigh impossible. By the end of the four days, my knee was seriously disabled, painful even when I was trying to sleep, and caused me a good deal of trouble for several months.

Despite the cold, lack of sleep, lack of food and the general strangeness – being worried that I would inadvertently offend some sensibility – I did not feel edgy or anxious, but quite tranquil much of the time. Though usually rather dependent on food, I didn't actually get hungry. Jodi, the guardian angel of the visitors, made it her mission to bring us each a hot soya drink from one of the stalls outside the *wat* each night, even in the pouring rain.

I learnt a lot about myself, and was able to learn a good deal about Thai Buddhism too. I did find it sexist: the monks, even the young boys, were arrogant and the nuns barely considered. When we had a general gathering one evening, the monks sat on a raised dais; at the front sat the male visitors, behind them the nuns, and behind them, the female visitors. We were there to repeat eight precepts including one against the use of bad language. So unmindful was I on leaving that I slipped down the wet marble steps, swearing "Shit" as I did so, and left my key in the door all night.

I also had a problem with any form of chanting – I do not repeat words that do not come from my heart – and especially with obeisance. On one occasion I was invited to share the leaving ceremony of another visitor. It took the form of an audience with the head monk, a much revered man called Ajahn Thong. To my horror, everyone began to prostrate themselves. I sat with eyes cast down, my hands together in a *wai*, and hoped I would not be noticed, though it was plain that the abbot's eyes were on me.

I later explained my predicament to my supervisor. I explained that Quakers have a testimony to equality which means we will not bow to any person, and that people had gone to prison in the seventeenth century for not taking their hats off to the king. My explanations were accepted – they would not have been happy with an explanation that spoke of mere pride on my part (though I confess now that pride did play a part!), and at my own leaving do I simply sat as I had done before. We were asked to reaffirm the eight precepts, but, since I was expected to carry away with me obedience to those principles, I only repeated those I was happy to live with. I did not, therefore, swear not to sing or dance, nor did I agree not ever to sleep on a high bed. But I did agree not to harm living creatures. I have since become a vegetarian and avoid killing insects, though I was interested to find that some of the monks and nuns ate meat.

Beth was an English nun whose cheerfulness and friendly smile came as a welcome contrast to the often sombre and reserved natures of the others. Her shaved head distinguished her from other Westerners, and her white skin from the other nuns. Although we were bidden to speak as little as possible, she entered freely into conversation with me on several occasions. She told me that she had originally come to the monastery to teach English, and had been invited to stay on to take orders. Her obedience as a nun did not lead her to be uncritical of what she found in the monastery. She felt that the sexism I had noticed was not inherent in Buddhism, but was an overlay from Thai culture. In Thailand nuns are not able to profess to the same level as monks. She was hoping for a transfer to Singapore or elsewhere where she could take further vows. Ajahn Thong was her direct supervisor, and she found the division between human being and establishment figure fascinating. She had little time for externals. She was also attracted by Daoism and planned to learn Mandarin, and see if she would be permitted to mix Buddhism with Dao.

I asked why she was attracted to Eastern religions. She said she was suspicious of anything smacking of Romanism, that the Eastern religions and languages had lasted for thousands of years and, while they were still there, she wanted to explore them. We talked of the authenticity of texts, of reincarnation, and made a brief mention of non-attachment – I had been astonished to discover that some of the nuns and monks were buying up new houses at the back of the monastery. Beth said darkly that that was not the only thing that would astonish me.

She had come across many Quakers among her parents' friends and had high regard for them. I, in my turn, could see the attractions of her monastic life. In many ways I am drawn to such a life, though as a hermit rather than in a community. I found the contact with her refreshing and important: an example of adventurous living at a profound level.

———

The only contacts we had in Thailand were on a list of isolated Friends that had been given us by Linley in New Zealand, and visiting them became our principal aim. As with all such lists, it was seriously out of date. Most people no longer existed at the addresses we had been given, though we did track down one, Don, by speaking to his ex-partner in the north of the country, who informed us he was now in Bangkok.

We had also promised to visit a friend of Stephen's Canadian cousin Marion. Karol, also a Canadian, lives in the north east, the poorest part of Thailand, in its second city, Nakhon Ratchasima (Khorat), where she teaches English at a Catholic school. The trains from Chiangmai had been fully booked for days so Stephen and I travelled on an overnight bus and met her at the school. She had been trained in acculturalisation by Franciscans and had been in Khorat for five months when we arrived. She was feeling very isolated, having no one of like mind to talk to, and being gently bullied by the local Thai women, who had a persistence beyond what we are used to, and to whom it was almost impossible to say no.

Karol feels called to live and work as a volunteer in the same conditions as her Thai colleagues under a draconian regime. They teach seven days a week, the only day off in a year being Christmas Day. The head teacher, a Catholic nun, pays them on a whim, sometimes at the end of the month, sometimes halfway through the next one, and the staff have to receive their pay on their knees. Karol lives in a flat among other teachers, without even a cooker. We slept on her settee overnight and held a Meeting for Worship with her, just the three of us. We had not realised that she had in the past attended Quaker

Meetings, but it turned out that when she lived in Honduras she flew over to a local island once a month, so great was her need to participate in Meeting. We told her of the international membership which exists to support isolated Friends, and advised her to apply.

Karol had on her dining room table a framed quote from Isaac Penington, one of the early Quakers:

Give over thine own willing

Give over thine own running

Give over thine own desiring to know or to be anything

And sink down to the seed which God sows in thy heart

And let it be in thy heart

And let it be in thee

And grow in thee

And breathe in thee

And act in thee

I learnt more from Karol about Thailand in a few minutes than from elsewhere in days. She confirmed the sense of unease I had been feeling with stories of appalling poverty, abandoned children and an epidemic of AIDS. She herself was feeding a child who camped out in a local shed. She talked of the complacency of the middle classes who know that such poverty exists, and take it as a given. She spoke of her own affluent married life on a large estate in Canada and how for many years after the break-up of her marriage she missed it. Now, in her totally changed life, she said she feels at home anywhere. She talked too of how she used to be content to "do good" then go home to her comfortable middle-class existence. Her life now is quite different, and difficult but, as she said, unlike her Thai colleagues, she has choices.

This conversation shook me. I was reminded of my unease at working in the East End while living comfortably elsewhere, an unease that I have never really resolved. Perhaps an aspect of this journey was a need to divorce myself from that comfortable home; to spend time alongside people in poverty, not cut myself off from them. In the meantime "home" was a rucksack and a hostel room – and that seemed OK.

"Glistening golden temples"

Bangkok, a city of seven million people and busy, noisy, traffic-ridden and vibrant, was more attractive than we had been led to believe. It was much cleaner than Cairo, for instance, and there were glimpses everywhere of glistening golden temples. We soon learnt to travel by boat, fast and cheap, on the wide muddy river. We stayed in a scruffy but clean and atmospheric guest house up a little cul de sac in an unfashionable part of town. A hangout for young backpackers, the area also had a reputation for drug dealing, and a number of the women serving at one of the local cafés were dressed in a way that is far from respectable in Thailand, in strappy tops and high heels. The alley or *soi*, dark and potentially dangerous, was fascinating in its cheek-by-jowl guest houses with ambiguous names, such as "Madam's", with rooms for "daily rent". I liked it: it was a community of women and children, with washing hung out in the street, a bird in a cage, and a couple of little shrines, which the owners tended and prayed to at sunset.

Noodles and rice were our staple diet, three times a day, plus fruit. Plenty of green veg with the noodles, breakfast usually soup at a local market stall which typically cost 45p for the two of us, mine 5p less because I didn't have chicken. It was good to be in a developing country again, and I liked the energy of Bangkok: especially China Town with all its stalls of smoking delicious-smelling food, and the streets of mechanics, mending machines of all descriptions. Workaday life.

But there is also an upwardly mobile section of the population that is leaving the others way behind, suggestive of a country in uncomfortable transition. On sale at a smart branch of Boots the Chemist in Bangkok were many of the items one would expect to find in Oxford Street or Leeds at prices way above what most Thais would be able to afford. As we left the shop I saw a young man pushing several cats and his obviously mentally deranged mother in a wheelbarrow with her few possessions. The gulf between such sections of the population was exemplified by the air-conditioned skytrain, clean, speedy, efficient and elegant. The carriages were full of smart uniformly dressed young men and women going to work; the train itself sped along rails high above the squalor and destitution of the other Bangkok.

Trat, a little southern town, is the jumping off point for islands in the Gulf of Thailand. It was also rather charming in its own right. It was a delight to be somewhere quieter than Bangkok, more Thai than Chiangmai – where tourism has come quite recently, and doesn't quite believe in itself, and the local people are unaffectedly friendly. Our guest house consisted of teak cabins on stilts, near the canal and the town centre. The rooms were generously proportioned, the bathrooms spotless. A double room cost £2 per night, and there was a nice sitting area where guests could and did chat. Many were longer-term residents – one a young Englishman who lives on the island of Ko Chang with his Thai girlfriend, another who runs a guest house in Cambodia. Quite a community.

Our aim was to get to Ko Wai, the quietest of the local islands, but we had to wait for a couple of days for a boat. We were a bit concerned about getting one back on the Saturday, in time to get back to Bangkok for the Meeting for Worship that we had organised. I was looking forward to another spell of tranquil idyllic living – the first since Tonga. It had proved hard to find an island unspoilt by tourist development. The gulf islands were being overtaken by more development every month, but habitués told us that Ko Wai was still unspoilt.

The next day, I was lulled asleep by the gentle motion as we crossed to the island in a workman-like wooden boat painted a rather unexpected pink. On board were Stephen, myself, the skipper, a young woman who was to cook for us, and a surly young German Swiss. Apparently he came every year, and seemed to resent our presence. The scene as we embarked was more like the Thailand I had imagined: pretty boats of various shapes and sizes, some chugging past, one with a woman in the stern, squatting as she prepared a meal, throwing the discarded matter into the water.

Paradise again.

A spacious rattan hut on a glorious island. There was little beach at high tide and a lot of flotsam from the recent high winds but a very beautiful shore line, irregular, occasionally rocky with palm trees waving in the breeze and a dense forested hinterland. We were served at meals by three transsexuals in long flowing skirts and cracked voices. We wondered whether they were in this out-of-the-way place because it was hard for them to be accepted in mainstream Thailand, or whether they would be part of the scenery anywhere we went.

We had been shocked on the way to Chiangmai a couple of weeks before when the train attendant collected up all the rubbish and calmly threw it out of the window. We saw something of the results of such actions on a windy day on the island as the stormy seas brought ashore not shells and starfish as in Tonga, but shampoo bottles and plastic bags. How will this country be in a few years' time?

We walked one day in the interior of the island on a thin path through tropical undergrowth, I nervous about snakes and wearing socks with my sandals, Stephen with boots and stick, every inch the intrepid explorer. When we reached the other shore we came upon a windless calm lagoon. We had been told that there was no indigenous population but we were pleased to find a couple with a dog living in an isolated little house. The man was not very friendly – I doubted they saw many visitors let alone *falangs* like us. Real jungle and our first sight of a rubber tree, slashed to collect the latex. I was reminded of my childhood in the Malaya of "the Troubles" and how dangerous the word "jungle" was when my father went out in it to find insurgents.

It was a good time on the island. And I was happy again, singing on the beach in the dark.

––––

Back in Bangkok, on Sunday morning we congregated at Don's penthouse apartment, which had a fine view of the city from windows on both sides of the sitting room. Crammed full of art and antiques, it was a luxurious place which he shared with his Thai partner, a young man whose family he had befriended. We had also invited a couple from the American Friends Service Committee, whom we had discovered were based in Bangkok. Karol too was due to join us from the north, but her car had broken down on the way.

Don, a man in his sixties or perhaps seventies, had had a fascinating career, working with anti-poverty and drugs programmes in New York and New Jersey, then running a restaurant in New York and a guest house in Northern Thailand. He had been in Thailand for 14 years, and told us of the great poverty he had come across, though more hidden than in India.

It was an example of the contradictions at the heart of Thailand that Don lived in this flat in a smart area largely inhabited by expats. In the shops near by could be found many of the foods without which Europeans and Americans feel deprived: Camembert, baguettes, smoked salmon and so on, and the meal we had in a nearby restaurant cost ten times what we normally paid at our noodle bars, though still only about £4 per head: a sophisticated meal of giant prawns and subtle spices. It was thoroughly enjoyable, but a million miles away from our little *soi* and Madam's Guest House.

––––

It was miles away too from Klong Prem men's prison, in the outskirts of Bangkok, which we reached the following day, ironically, by skytrain and taxi. Linley had given us names of prisoners asking to be visited, and we also had a list of British prisoners given to us by the British consul. We put ourselves down to visit Joe, our first prisoner, went through the security processes, leaving our bags behind, and sat down to wait. Inside the gates, the surroundings of the prison buildings were pretty, with benches in spacious gardens, and there were a number of other people, mostly women and children, some with large bundles that they gave to the guards to take in to their relations.

We met two remarkable women there. One was a Thai prison visitor, working on behalf of a priest, Father Olivier, and the Catholic Church. She asked us if we would also visit an Algerian who had no contacts in the city – she had too many on her list for the day. The other was Debbie, a young Englishwoman living in Perth, Australia, whose brother was in the prison, serving ten years for passing a dud travellers cheque. We caught sight of him fleetingly: he was a handsome blond young man, who had now contracted TB. I felt an impatience with him, a man from an affluent background whose action had not only ruined years of his life but meant that his sister and mother had to make the expensive journey from Perth every six months to visit him.

However, the experience has certainly opened Debbie's eyes. She now visits other prisoners when she is over, and brings boxes of books for them. She is also collecting reading glasses – the extension of a scheme in Australian prisons. We were drawn to each other, and have stayed in touch.

The visiting area itself was outside an L-shaped building, with a long line of seats in front of meshed windows behind which the prisoners filed in to sit, some of them in chains. What must it be like for a small child to see his father with chains on his legs? Apparently the conditions in the prison, despite recent improvements, are pretty grim: four to six in a cell, sleeping on the ground with a blanket. Very little food unless they can afford an extra payment.

All the men we visited were reasonably sanguine, the least being Joe. He said he had been tortured in Burma, and did not get the medication he needed. He had one year of his sentence to go and was seeking asylum. We spoke to the Catholic visitor, and asked if she could help – she said that Father Olivier did arrange for medicaments to be brought to prisoners and was fairly sure Joe was on his list.

We were concerned to find that we were officially only allowed to visit one prisoner a day, but as the staff had changed when we went back to reception we went ahead and registered to visit Iyke. He is a Nigerian who has served 12 years with another eight-and-a-half years to go, unless his country signs a treaty with Thailand. Intelligent and articulate, he said he had learnt a lot in prison, and was attending English classes run by Debbie's brother. Iyke felt very cut off, as his family was too poor even to buy stamps to write to him. We promised to write but urged him not to spend his money on writing to us. However, when we arrived in India a month later, my son brought a letter from him in which he said that our visit had made that day the best in the whole time he had been in prison. One hour's visit had meant so much in a life of such deprivation. There is now some chance that he will be repatriated to serve the rest of his time in a Nigerian prison, but he needs money for the fare and some clothes.

When we went back to register a third time, we were told we could not. I pleaded – we would not be coming again; this was our one chance – and in the end the official relented. Tewfiq, the Algerian whom we visited next, said he had been mentally ill with the shock of being imprisoned, and had been badly beaten by the guards when he was unable to work. He was very bitter about the Thais and their inhumanity – called them animals. He had not yet been sentenced, and had been waiting for 18 months. Father Olivier is going to look into his case – we seemed always to be referring problems to him: our only contact with enough power and know-how to get things done.

I think the prisoners welcomed our visit. It was hard to relate, the mesh through which we talked hiding the face of the man opposite. Only when we stood up to leave did we see him clearly through the glass. We ordered some food and toiletries for each of them, then went to eat in the canteen which had a voucher system that we simply could not understand. My inability to make myself understood brought tears of frustration to my eyes. Having missed breakfast, and having been at the prison since 8.30 a.m., we were tired by mid-afternoon, and Stephen was not at all well.

Complaining of back pains as well as a sore throat, he had asked me to massage him the previous day, and I had found a big rash. It looked like shingles to me, but the doctor he had seen thought differently and had given him some pills for the different symptoms. He was later diagnosed with shingles, warned that he would be in great pain for months, given the right drug immediately, and – to our amazement and relief – the disease did not develop.

The following day we left for India.

I had never quite managed to come to terms with Thailand – perhaps we didn't manage to get to the right places – but in a way I think my unease was a response to a country itself ill at ease with its own development, with the gulf between rich and poor, and between traditional Buddhist culture and its increasing Westernisation. A small minority of the population has moved into another century, leaving the vast majority behind. The gap between rich and poor exists in most countries of the world, including the UK, but seems particularly stark in this halfway house between first and third worlds. The tourist trade is more established here than in other parts of South-East Asia, and it has had a deleterious effect, challenging the traditional ways of its own people. We were of course aware of the iniquities of the sex trade, and were made aware of a strange discrepancy between a perceived latitude about drug taking, and the draconian punishments meted out to those who are caught.

Although we did not encounter examples of the sex trade, there was an undercurrent we had not come across before, and the general type of tourists that we met there seemed quite different from those we had encountered in other parts of the world. In Latin America, we had met delightful young people searching for authentic cultures, many of them volunteering for schools, hospitals and orphanages; in India we were to meet people on spiritual quests, moving, as we were, from one ashram to another. Here, however, there was more a sense of people out for what they could get, living off people poorer than themselves. In Bangkok, the guests in the hotels near ours were older and often longer-term, somewhat louche. I heard one such, a Frenchman, accost the owner of "Madam's" in broken English: "You people, you make all your money from beer and people fucking little girls and boys."

CHAPTER 11

Converging Paths

The humble, meek, merciful, just, pious and devout souls are everywhere of one religion; and when death has taken off the mask they will know one another, though the divers liveries they wear here makes them strangers

William Penn, in *Quaker Faith and Practice*

How can one begin to write about India? For me, from the kaleidoscope of experience during the three months that we were there – the travel by train where every moment outside was a snapshot of vivid varied village life or glimpse of landscape; all the colour; the dignity and beauty of the women, however poor; the cows wandering nonchalantly through the traffic, the beggars, the smells, car horns, swindling auto taxis, earnest conversations on trains – from all this richness emerged the deep spirituality of the country which imbues it at all levels. I had never understood why people felt they had to go to India to find their spiritual identities; more appropriate, I have always thought, to find a faith that related to their own culture.

An early encounter confirmed me in this view. Soon after we reached India, my son, Guy, arrived to spend Christmas with us. He had not come so far to spend his holiday in cold climes, so we all headed down to Kerala, in the far south of India, to spend a happy hot week in Fort Cochi. On the way, we decided to break the 48-hour journey and spend the night in the small and unremarkable town of Kannur. I remembered that this was the town of the swami that my mother meets in London, and thought Stephen and I should make the effort to meet him. He kindly suggested taking us to his new (second) ashram that he was due to visit that day and picked us up in his chauffeur-driven car. He spent much of the day with us, introducing us to his mother who looks after him, and showing us with great pride the seven-and-a-half hectare grounds of the ashram and the homeopathic clinic that is available to all local people for a nominal annual fee.

The swami was a stocky, good-looking bubbly man in his thirties, with big frizzy black hair and beard, and very large expressive eyes. He came from a poor family and said he had known his destiny from childhood. He related his miracles and cures with childlike pleasure – no false modesty here – but also laid his hands on our heads in prayer and healing. It was peaceful there, and Stephen was able to meditate. We promised to donate to the ashram on our return. The swami was full of natural wisdom, and was revered in many countries of the world, but I knew that his way was not for me. The intervention of a human being in the relationship with God is for me acutely uncomfortable, especially when the human being in question accepts his worship with equanimity. But I admired his achievements and his acceptance of all castes and religions.

We only visited one Quaker Meeting in India, a gathering of two or three souls in a central YWCA in Delhi, keen to expand its outreach and its attendance. As we travelled round the country, we returned often to Delhi, and its Meeting became a focus for our worship. An oasis of stillness in the clangour of the city.

What I had not understood before coming to India was that it was not necessarily a particular religion that people go to find, rather to breathe in the spiritual oxygen. I had first come across this phenomenon in Bangladesh three years before: where eye contact with women I was visiting in the slums became a wordless exchange of common humanity and womanhood. India is a more sophisticated country but religion still pervades daily life and governs the way people live.

For me there were two important affirmations in India – two areas of spiritual life that touched closely my own beliefs and practices. The roots of Quakerism are in Christianity but many of us feel that we have moved away from calling ourselves Christians; that we do not wish to assert that any path to God is superior. We have a strong tradition of welcoming people from all religions. We have Jewish Quakers, Buddhist Quakers, Quakers from all the major faiths, and joint membership is not unusual. My own faith is strongly universalist: for me, as for many, what religions have in common is far more important than their differences, which are often the externals, rituals or cultural accretions. There was a current running through our encounters with both Indians and those who have chosen to live there, of a willingness to combine the best of faiths, to borrow from other faiths, most of all of a recognition that all faiths resemble each other at their mystic core, in those things that are eternal.

Stephen's main desire in India, indeed almost in the whole trip, was to visit Saccandinanda Santivanam ashram in Tamil Nadu, South India. It was one of the first Christian ashrams in India, originally set up in the 1950s by two Belgian Benedictine monks, and taken over by a British monk from Prinknash, Bede Griffiths, by whose name it is generally known. Christianity is widespread in India: in fact there are more Christians – some 20 million – than Sikhs. What made the founding of Santivanam ("Sacred Mango Grove") exceptional was that its mission was not to impose Catholicism on Hindus, or an English style on an Indian community, but to bring together the different traditions; unconventionally, especially at that time, to absorb much of Indian and Hindu into what is essentially a Catholic monastery. Reading Bede Griffiths, seeing him on video, I identified with his movement away from a particular faith to one embracing all. He saw in a strand of modern Hinduism a universal truth to which he could relate, and we found the same.

Father Bede died some years ago, and with him has gone some of the depth of spiritual ecumenism, but the ashram still retains enough of a mixture of cultures to be inspiring. The Benedictine monks dress in the clothes of *saddhus* or holy men; the church is designed like a Hindu temple, with brightly coloured statues on top, but of Christian figures, not Hindu gods; the services include Sanskrit and Tamil chanting as well as the psalms in English, the Eucharist and other Catholic features. We spent two weeks there, eating simple and delicious vegetarian food communally and in silence, sitting on the floor and eating with our right hands.

Even with the constant flow of guests that come from all over the world, Santivanam is a quiet, reflective place that Stephen in

Santivanam: graves of the founders, including Father Bede

particular found enormously enriching. I found myself often dry and frustrated in attempting to fit into a religious life that was not mine. Believing that all of life is sacramental and that no particular time or season is more significant or holy than another, I found myself resistant to attending regular services in the church. I did however attend the meditation periods at 6 a.m. and 6 p.m., though the mosquitoes, at their peak at those times, made concentration in that open-sided church difficult. I often migrated to the meditation hall, which had a cool marble floor and – oh, wonder – a fan!

As I increasingly realised, it is often by the natural world that my spirit is liberated: I wrote in my journal on January 2nd:

> *We have been given a hut, as we are staying for a while. I feel very privileged. It is set apart a little with its own bathroom, facing on to a field of trees and across a lane along which people cycle to other fields and, in the distance, other trees. A little porch where I sit on a wicker chair in a cool evening breeze. What more could one want? (Except that I have just been bitten by a ferocious red ant.) There's even a welcoming chalk pattern at the entrance, though not, I gather, specifically for us. But it feels as if it is.*

Here, at the edge of the ashram, I saw just now a tussle between a tiny striped squirrel and a pair of handsome squawking birds, big, nut brown with white stripe. The squirrel, same size as the birds, won.

Oh such a kingfisher! I looked up from my chair and there he was, sitting on a little branch. Brown with a white bib and a slash of brilliant turquoise at the side. I looked for many minutes. Then he turned, briefly showing a breathtaking turquoise back, swooped to pick up an insect and flew off, so brilliant, such a gift. I had been feeling cross and, as so often, I felt as if I had been sent a messenger, a present of beauty.

Such experiences were a confirmation of my ministry being in the world, in allowing my spirit to expand into the whole world; confining it in highly disciplined rituals of meditation had a depressing effect, did not make use of all of God's grace. Uniting with the created universe is heady, liberating, enabling. I had felt it in the desert, in the Andes; I felt it daily on this journey when I allowed it to happen. It was good to recognise it in myself – each path is different, and we need to find our own.

One day, Stephen and I went for a walk after breakfast along a woody path parallel with the river. It was a walk, as often, punctuated by the bodily functions of local inhabitants: a pungent smell and a man appearing out of the woods; another standing in the river in his underpants, soaping himself; a third pedalling purposefully towards the river, toothbrush between his teeth. Beside the path an abundance of butterflies came out to sun themselves and drink from the white flowers: a large pale blue and black, many varieties of smaller orange and two large black ones, one with deep velvety red, the other an equally opulent blue. And last of all came a tiny jewel with rich blue crosses turning purple as its wings closed. I felt such a thirst for this beauty, and a need to adore in silence.

I spent a good deal of time talking to, and learnt a lot from, one of the other visitors: an Englishman, Gyan, who had lived for many years in India, shaved his head, and often wore the saffron *dhoti* of the *saddhus*. A tall handsome man in, perhaps, his late forties, he swam in the river near the ashram most days that we were there. He was pleasingly irreverent, as well as gentle with his fellow human beings, and often supplied some welcome light relief. He told me of a silent retreat he had attended some years ago in Australia. A friend of his passed him a note which said, "Are we being silent, or are we trying not to talk?" Though he now lives in Italy, running a yoga centre with his partner, Gyan is still very close to his Indian experience and is a prime example of a spiritual man not needing to attach himself to a single named faith or to possessions. He told us that he had never owned much and had no insurances or pension: living in the present, like the lilies in the field. I asked if he had not found it difficult to leave his cell and come back into the world. He answered: "I carry it with me."

Gyan was able to shed some light on a remarkable event. At the end of the lane running alongside the boundary of the ashram beside our hut was a local meeting point with a brick shelter. One day we heard a lot of singing and banging of drums and tambourines and saw a procession coming down the lane, with a garlanded cart. We had seen just such a scene on a Bede Griffiths video the previous night, so we recognised it as a Hindu funeral. Stephen and I did not feel we could intrude, particularly in my case, since all the procession – one could not call them mourners – were male. But we looked on from the step of our hut and could see that the body had been placed in the shelter – the crematorium, it seemed – and, after some incantations and prayers, it was smeared with mud, sprinkled with what Gyan told us were coconut juice and hay and set alight. We did not venture past it for a day or so, but for some time the pungent smell drifted over the fields and into our hut. Gyan told us that such ceremonies are carried out wherever there is a river, often many in a day. He recounted gruesome stories of how bits of bodies are left unburnt, and devoured by the stray dogs of the neighbourhood.

I had little to do with the nuns, who did not live on the premises, but I was keen to visit Sister Stephanie, who lived as a hermit near by. We travelled to her home by bus, and were startled to find quite a big house with large grounds. The main building housed a chapel and several rooms, one of which was occupied by Father Martin, the most intellectual of the brothers at Santivanam. He was on sabbatical at the time, though he travelled abroad a lot to lecture. (Indeed, we attended one of his talks on our return to England.) Sister Stephanie's home in a separate building was under repair, so she too was living in the main house. There were several staff, a cow and a lot of activity. Not my idea of a hermitage.

While we sipped tea, Stephen asked Stephanie, "What is the difference between living alone and being a hermit?" The million dollar question.

She paused then said, "Silence in the heart. That is the true hermitage, the hermitage of the heart."

A day or so later, I had a brief word with Father Ivan, the Italian monk at Santivanam, over tea. His was a sharply defined face with a little beard and big eyes. He often smiled a greeting to the cook, to me, and to others, but his general demeanour was serious and withdrawn. I sensed a keen intelligence and a devout spirit. Here, I felt, was a man who might teach me something. He was visiting the ashram to verify the implementation of policies agreed by delegates of the Camaldoli monasteries to which Santivanam is allied.

When I expressed the problem of adapting to a totally interior life, he said it was the same for them – even when withdrawn from the world, there was the problem of remaining "conscious" in word and deed. I said that with no words, as in Quaker practice, when there was nothing, there was, well, nothing, and he laughed.

I repeated Sister Stephanie's phrase of the "silence in the heart". He thought for a while then said,

"Maybe that is because it has a breath in it, a presence." Yes.

I was increasingly attracted by the idea of eremitic living. After a lifetime of trying to fit in with those I lived with, perhaps it was time to live alone. Certainly emotional turmoil played havoc with the interior life that was becoming increasingly important to me. I recalled an Englishwoman I had met on a Quaker course who had expressed the intention of becoming a solitary, and thought I might visit her on my return.

After visiting Sister Stephanie I had an appointment with the inhabitant of the next hut to ours. Father Augustine is an elderly and infirm Indian monk who has been at Santivanam for a number of years. He husbands his energies carefully and did not appear often at the regular tea- and coffee-time meeting points. He had showed us great warmth in all our meetings, but had not felt strong enough for a long encounter until this moment. It was hot, but he sat in a woollen cap and waistcoat, anxious not to be in a draught as we held a wide-ranging conversation on prayer and doubt, with constant references from Father Augustine to Jesus' life as a guide. I told him that I had been growing in the realisation that meditation in the form of a sterile emptying of the mind was not for me. I found that when I approached a centred state prayerfully, lovingly, I fell into it peacefully, without noticing. This process was more like that in a Meeting for Worship – and indeed, I now recognised that there could only be one kind of relationship with God, not two different modes. Father Augustine told me that what I had described – prayer leading to contemplation – is a recognised procedure in Christian practice, though I do not feel myself to be a Christian.

During my time at Santivanam, my mind was often on my father, who became a Catholic when I was five, and who was also diagnosed a schizophrenic at about that time. My life at the ashram was so like his – praying and reading all day, often prostrate and tired. How cross we used to be at his "laziness". He wanted to become a monk later on in life, and they would not have him, both because he was married, and because of his history of mental illness. But as I lived among those who had been accepted into that life that he craved, I felt his pain, rejection and frustration. No wonder he thought of himself as Job.

A book I was reading challenged me to pray for what I really wanted and felt, not what I thought I ought to want and feel. It was true. All my life I had been so duty bound, I had hidden my real wishes from myself. A second book bid me stop playing games with myself, and let the inner and the outer become one. Part of the same thing from two different sources.

It was at Santivanam that Stephen and I started a study of modern Hinduism that has continued. From our reading there and later, we learnt of a whole tradition of Hinduism that was far from the general understanding in the West of a polytheistic faith verging on the superstitious. Brahmo Samaj (the Society of God), founded in 1828 by a Bengali Brahmin, Ram Mohan Roy, and taken up by the father of the poet Rabindranath Tagore, rejected that polytheism and emphasised the importance of the formless universal spirit: the monotheistic basis of Hinduism and its links with other faiths. I had always found it hard to equate what I read from the Upanishads and Bhagavad Gita with what I saw in the multifarious images of Hindu temples in England and in India. It was good to understand that Vishnu, Shiva, Kali, or Ganesh could be seen as entry points to the deeper mystical faith behind.

As we moved from ashram to ashram in the south and east of the country, often recommended by other "pilgrims", we found ourselves in a universalist Hindu tradition that included such figures as Ramakrishna, whose centre we visited in Delhi, Vivekananda, Sri Ramana and Sri Aurobindo. From all we felt a spiritual charge, and a recognition of the similarities of our faith. From an anthology, *The Power of Prayer*, Swami Swahananda's comment that "group prayer is not an aggregate but a symphony" might have been a description of a Quaker Meeting for Worship.

At these ashrams we did not recapture the feeling of community that we had felt at Santivanam. At Tiruvanamali, for instance, an ashram devoted to Sri Ramana, there were a lot of Westerners wandering about, chatting, and very little silence, ironic since the sage himself, it appears, preferred to communicate through the power of silence, a silence so profound that it stilled the minds of those who came to visit him. Something of that silence remained in the small whitewashed cave where he lived; we climbed up to it, and contemplated its serenity.

The ashram was all much bigger, spread out and less intimate than we had been used to, though redeemed by the glorious peacocks on the roof and by the less glorious monkeys who tried to get into our room. Stephen had bought a *dhoti* and wore it with aplomb, though it took time to learn how to sit on the ground at mealtimes without revealing all. What a transformation from a man wedded to his boots and socks.

A number of the visitors seemed somewhat self-conscious. It is hard for Westerners to look good in Indian clothes, especially when compared with the beauty and elegance of Indian women. The clothes simply don't hang well on our different shapes and gaits. But some, including a delicate French woman dressed always in white, had been in India a long time – five years in her case – and seemed completely at home.

While we were at Tiruvanamali, I heard of a job in the UK that would have been just up my street: part of the organisation I had been working for, but looking at microcredit in a European context. If I had still been in "career" mode, it would have been the natural next step for me. As it was, I knew that I must keep myself free until my return. Still, temptation would not be temptation if it were not attractive, just as faith would not be necessary if everything could be known for sure.

After some time in the library I found myself sated with guru literature, partly because I disliked the devotion shown to human beings, and partly because all the analysis did not help, rather it impeded me. Having read summaries and hand-picked examples of Hindu mystical thought in Huxley and other anthologies, none of what I was now reading seemed very fresh. *Doing* it is what is important, and hard, and I found that my resistance to some of this reading was contributing to my resistance to letting go in meditation.

We bumped into Frs George and Ivan from Santivanam, who were also staying in the ashram. George was so much more relaxed away from his responsibilities, with a smile of greeting from the heart and through the eyes. We also met again Klaske, a young Dutch woman who has set up home in India, not far from Dharamsala, and devotes her life to spiritual practices. When I asked her whether she was a Buddhist, she said, "Oh, I'm not anything."

I said, "Oh, you mean you are everything." And tendered for the first time the possibility that I too could be everything. We don't need a name or a label, or to fit into a pigeonhole: our faith is our own.

I was moving on. The Spirit is dynamic; we do not believe today exactly what we believed yesterday, which is why Quakers have no creed. We are on a journey and things of the past may not work in the present. It was brought home to me by re-reading *Ordinary People as Monks and Mystics*. I had greeted it with such passion a few months before in the States; now it hardly resounded at all.

Is the Divine the supreme fact of your life, so much so that it is simply impossible for you to do without it? . . . This is the first thing necessary – aspiration for the Divine. The next thing you have to do is to tend it, to keep it always alert and awake and living. And for that what is required is concentration – concentration upon the Divine with a view to an integral and absolute consecration to its Will and Purpose.

The Mother

Mary is an Englishwoman who has lived in the Sri Aurobindo Ashram in the French town of Pondicherry for the last thirty years – she is also a member of our own Quaker Meeting. Mary is 92 and is a delicate mixture of forgetful old age and a spiritual being wrapped in silence. She lives in an ashram flat, receiving all her food from the ashram kitchens. She is surrounded by photos of Sri Aurobindo and his disciple, the French woman known as The Mother, with whom she had several private silent audiences. Mary spends much of her time in meditation, but feels very connected to her Quaker Meeting, and was much moved by the Meeting for Worship that we held in her flat. It was the first she had attended since her last visit to Britain some ten years before.

We talked gently of important subjects. Mary believes firmly in reincarnation; I am more sceptical. But our spiritual journeys move on, and who knows what we will feel about it in six months' time. The little that I had managed to read of a book by Henri Le Saux (Abhishiktananda), one of the founders of Santivanam, was so revealing in its detailing in journal form the process, the changes in his spiritual life; how, in very human terms, he "got to" the position of *sanyasi* in later life. For once here was an account that rendered the possibilities in our own journeys comprehensible.

Meeting Mary reminded me of Father Bede who said at the age of 86 that he had learned more in the last two years than in the previous 84, and of my mother, the same age, to whom I had recounted it, to cheer her. Later Mary wrote: "No doubt it is too much to ask for you to come and give us another visit? But if you do . . . then our arms are waiting for you!" A year later Westminster Monthly Meeting recorded her death.

Pondicherry vibrates with the influence of Sri Aurobindo and The Mother; their photos are everywhere, and much of the town is owned by the ashram – to the extent, apparently, that it is more influential than the town council. We stayed in an ashram guest house and took breakfast and dinner with other visitors and monks in the dining area, but I did not feel part of any community. I couldn't identify either with what I saw as the idolatry of those prostrating themselves at the graves of Aurobindo and The Mother. It seemed out of kilter with their teachings. Many years ago, another visitor, disturbed by this worship of the then living Mother, wrote to her and asked, "Mother, are you God?"

"Yes," she replied, "and so are you."

I also felt uncomfortable at living in all these ashrams without being given any voluntary work to do. At Santivanam at least we had been able to help each day. I had prepared the vegetables for lunch, and Stephen cleaned out the cow shed. It was a shame that none of the other ashrams seemed to include useful activity as part of their ethos.

Another discomfort was an insight while walking down the road to the ashram. After watching with delight a pair of beautiful butterflies, I became aware of a far from beautiful boy at my side – dirty, unkempt, downcast. I barely noticed him, and passed on. It was only later that I realised how little attention I had given him, indeed had been giving to all destitute human beings in India – how little beauty I saw in them. I felt I had left behind my understanding of and empathy with the excluded. In England, though I do not give money, I buy food, have a conversation. Here I was doing nothing – I could not converse, of course – and was passing by on the other side. At Tiruvanamali I had witnessed the daily feeding of the poor: a sobering long queue of *saddhus*, holy men who depend on charity, but also indigenous local poor, receiving a large bowlful of rice. As I ate another generous meal I couldn't help feeling the imbalance: it should have been we who received the one bowl of rice, and the poor our three good meals a day.

A few miles from Pondicherry is Auroville, an area of 15 square miles given over to an international community, which was set up in the 1960s by The Mother "to be the first realisation of human unity based on the teaching of Sri Aurobindo, where men of all countries would be at home". With its luxurious café with newspapers and internet facilities, it did not feel like India – it could almost have been in Covent Garden. We found ourselves in an expensive guest house, a delightful leafy enclave of middle-class visitors, some of them considering the possibility of joining the community. Though everyone was perfectly pleasant, I felt ill at ease, out of our usual environment.

We had come to visit Joss, an Australian Quaker forester who is one of the founder members of the community, and who had joined us in Meeting for Worship with Mary. The distances are great and there is no public transport to the spread-out residences, so we hired a scooter (aagh!) for less than £1 and went off to visit Joss and his wife, Anita, for lunch. They run a fascinating project, an important strand of which is the education of local women about herbal medicine; growing and attempting to reintroduce the herbs into local communities that have lost touch with their traditions. We also rode off to visit Bob, a back specialist, who treated Stephen and gave me some advice about my knee, but declined payment. Members of the community, it seems, only ask for donations. Bob mentioned that Pondicherry attracted strange events (Saturn's influence, he said), and that it was possible that Stephen's back problem and the pain in my knee were results of being there.

At the centre of this town is the vast meditation centre planned by The Mother, and not yet completed, called the Matrimandir. In the queue was Gyan. It was good to see him again, and he was amused at our ailments. Echoing Bob, he said, "India is obviously good for you and Stephen; you are getting the reactive ailments."

I explained the possible physical reasons.

"You're right," said he mockingly, "it's not spiritual."

Before being allowed to meditate at Matrimandir one has to join the vast queue of mostly Indian people who come simply to see it as a tourist attraction. It's a frustrating experience, full of form-filling, all for a few seconds' glimpse of the interior. However, once having passed that test of patience, one is allowed a pass to enter for meditation. And it was worth the effort. In a vast golden globe centred round an enormous crystal, the white marble hall provides an atmosphere of electric purity, a huge cavern of soundlessness. A place, as The Mother said, "for trying to find one's consciousness".

Sometimes my respect for Indian customs wore thin – especially when one of our companions on the train persistently spat long-distance into a far corner. What I chiefly found difficult was the expected servility of women: the way our hostess in an enlightened middle-class family served us and her husband first (referring to him throughout as Mr), standing behind us to deal with our every wish; a couple on the next seats to us in the train, in their sixties, not exchanging a word, eating continually, she serving him at every moment.

One day, as we got on a bus in Delhi, a young Muslim was taking up a seat for two and I asked him courteously if he would move up. He stared at me, blank-faced. I realised that it was culturally not appropriate for him to move for a woman and tactfully indicated to Stephen that he should sit there; the young man immediately moved up. It was only later that I felt incensed. Who did that jumped-up little twerp think he was?!

Now, as we travelled on a local train from Kolkata (Calcutta) to Chandanaggar, standing, pressed together with the elbows of fellow travellers in our ribs (shades of rush hour on the Northern Line), I was once again uncomfortably aware of my femaleness: despite modest clothing, male eyes were always on me, bodies pressed against me, not always accidentally. A white woman was enough of a novelty for provincial men to find me fascinating.

Chandanaggar was an oasis of peace. Like Pondicherry, it is a French town and had had a brief spell as an independent city state, between its time with colonial status and when it became part of the rest of India. We travelled to our host's home by three-wheeler bicycle taxi, gliding silently along the broad streets, among other cycles, hardly a car in sight, barely a sound to be heard. And there we had our first sight of the Ganga river, Mother India.

Our host, Viswenath Singha Roy, had visited me in England a year or so before we set off on our travels. Margaret, a mutual friend and British Quaker who has spent a lot of time in India, brought him to my flat to have tea. He was involved with the introduction of microcredit in some projects in India, and they wondered whether I could be of any help. So I arrived in Chandanaggar in expectation of some focused work at last.

Vishy lives with his wife, Lipika, and two teenage children, Sharmistra and Subesh, in a small vertical house with a roof garden. Despite our protests, we slept in the main bedroom; the family shared a large bed and small camp bed in the sitting room. Owners of a more substantial house in the country, they were renting this house in town for the duration of their children's schooling. They had a "houseboy", a man who is like one of the family. Almost destitute, he had been given this job, earned some self-respect, and was thus able to feed his wife and family.

It was a delightful household; a civilised and educated family with generous open hearts. They were devout Hindus: Lipika and Sharmistra performed their *puja* (shrine worship) every evening, and both blew the haunting conch shell at sunset. Their particular household goddess was Sarasvati, the goddess of knowledge and music, a statue of whom Stephen bought me for my birthday.

Vishy is a small man with a thin face, long hair and an immense enthusiasm that revived it in Stephen. The two of them joked and larked about like two children for much of the time we were together. Indians are reticent about relations between members of the opposite sex, and frown on any demonstration of affection, even holding hands in the street. Between men, however, it is quite usual to see displays of affection, holding hands, embracing, sitting on each other's laps. Vishy's natural inclination was to be demonstrative with Stephen, who, a true Anglo-Saxon, found it hard when Vishy held his hand, and tried to interpolate me between them as we walked along the road.

Vishy works as an international fundraiser and generator of ideas for two charities, and is also employed by the government as an inspector of NGOs. If there is a complaint against an NGO, he and one or two others go to look at the charity and see if there is any basis in the complaint. It is an extremely responsible job, and it is only because he is a man of the utmost integrity that he has been chosen.

He told us of an occasion some years before when he had been sent to a poor village to look at a water project. The village lake – the water supply for the village – was meant to be passed into the official ownership of the villagers. Instead, it became clear that the village chief was gradually processing documentation for ownership for himself. On arrival at the village, Vishy asked him for his accounts.

"How much do you want?"

"I don't want anything," said Vishy, "except your accounts on my desk by the end of the week."

The man prevaricated and a few days later Vishy became suspicious when all the staff in the house that had been assigned to him asked for the evening off. He had by then made himself popular with local villagers, so he alerted them to the fact that he would be alone in the house that evening. So when late that night several armed men turned up on motorbikes, the local residents came round in force and drove the men away. Finally all the proof of the fraud was in Vishy's hands. The chief came to him, and begged him to let him off, said that he would be ruined, pleaded not to be sent to gaol. Vishy said that it wasn't up to him, that he would have to hand him over to the village. A village meeting was called, at which the chief was utterly humiliated, but was allowed to leave without being further punished. The villagers felt that he had suffered enough.

Our expectation was that we would get a chance to roll up our sleeves and muck in. Far from it. We were driven in one of the ubiquitous white Ambassador cars – embarrassingly, with VIP plates on it – to Ramagiri, the headquarters of ISARA. This was one of the NGOs that Vishy advised, an organisation which works on a variety of projects with hill tribe people. As we drove, Vishy broke into song – astonishingly, evangelical Christian hymns such as "I Have Been Washed in the Blood of the Lamb".

I was amused, then realised that he was completely in earnest. It turned out that he had worked for some years for US Aid, with a group of evangelical Christians, and these hymns and the Bible became part of the fabric of his faith. He broke into songs of this kind throughout our two weeks with him and although I cringed at the sentimentality of the tunes and lyrics, and sometimes light-heartedly asked him to desist, his faith was such that it completely won us over. He was a deeply spiritual man – conversations with him sometimes felt like a religious service. I agreed wholeheartedly with him about the beauty and fundamental importance of the Beatitudes – they are quite central to life and faith. For the first time I understood the strength of phrases that before had seemed superficial and facile. If taken away from its normal context, even "born again" is beautiful.

We found out later that Vishy had become a Baptist in the 1990s, his baptism causing a great deal of trouble in the family. The seventh son of a seventh son, it was unacceptable for him to leave his faith for another, and he was deprived of his lands and even, for a time, of his wife. When they came back together again it was agreed that the children would attend Catholic schools.

Men of integrity such as Vishy are not rare, even in a country where corruption is rife. Nor, as we found, are people who devote their lives to the service of others. What I found interesting about Vishy, apart from his engaging cheerfulness and positive attitude to life, was his conversion to a faith so different from his original one. He sees no contradiction between the traditional Hinduism of his family and his own Christianity.

From all such encounters it was clear that Quakers are not alone in their universalist tendencies. I was excited by these conjunctions of faith; by the recognition not only that there are many paths, but that they can run alongside or even join together for much of the way.

Gandhi, for whom interfaith reconciliation was a crucial part of his mission, was interested in the role of Quakerism in such a union. A friend of his proposed the founding of a

> *religious fellowship which can be and will be joined by adherents of all the chief religions. I am not thinking of a syncretistic movement like Theosophy, which deliberately tries to take the best of each faith and joins them together. I am thinking of a union of hearts, a fellowship in which men of each faith, Hindu, Buddhist, Parsi, Jew, Muslim, Christian, all find themselves at one . . . And I wondered whether the Society of Friends, the "Quakers" so called, could help to provide such a meeting ground.*

Gandhi's response was to ask if Quakers would be prepared to *"recognise that it is as natural for a Hindu to grow into a Friend as it is for a Christian to grow into one"*. Many of us do. That is the whole point of the universalist position.

CHAPTER 12

Service as Worship

True godliness don't turn men out of the world but enables them to live better in it and excites their endeavours to mend it

William Penn, in *Quaker Faith and Practice*

*C*hristians and Quakers tend to think they have a monopoly on "good works", on the notion of service as worship. It is true that something about Quakerism has traditionally led people into action. It may be something to do with the do-it-yourself nature of the Society. We have no paid priests; we take responsibility for our faith and for the running of our organisation. Maybe that has led us to take responsibility for the state of the world: "If not me, then who?" It also comes, I think, out of the Meeting for Worship itself. The movement of love in our hearts impels us to express it in our relationships with other human beings. A belief in the Spirit leads to an enabling culture, which does not demand qualifications or experience from someone who is inspired to act.

But one of our principal discoveries in India was that Hindus also believe and practise service as worship, to a humbling degree. Sri Aurobindo, in particular, stressed the importance of work. Like William Penn, he felt that godliness was expressed in one's work in the world, that old traditions of monastic life were missing the point, that the purification advocated by Hinduism and other faiths was a stage to be reached in order to serve God better in the world.

Our first experience of voluntary work in India was in a charity school about a hundred kilometres outside Delhi and a pet project of a Quaker friend of Stephen's. We duly reported for duty, and were billeted, to our delight, with the headmistress, Kamla, in a little house complete with monkeys.

Kamla comes from a highly educated family. Originally from

the Islamabad area of what is now Pakistan, she had to leave college just before Partition and for safety's sake moved to Kashmir. Kamla is a mathematician with a master's degree from London University, and had been teaching at one of India's elite schools. A non-practising Hindu, she felt impelled to move to the provincial town of Sohna in Haryana Province, and live in a much smaller house with very basic facilities, in order to start up the school and charitable foundation. Now, at 73, she is tired, and longs for a successor to appear.

I talked to Kamla about her motivation. She says she doesn't feel she has a choice; that although she does not practise or talk about religion, she feels called "by something outside" herself. She is a scientist and an intellectual. She does not have much time for gurus who are worshipped for their "magic tricks" and don't appear to have anything new to say. The attraction of Hinduism for her is that it enables individuals to worship in the way they think best, that it does not dictate practices but encourages choice. Like many Quakers and other Hindus that we met, she feels that the way of life is what matters.

Sangam School is a fascinating educational experiment. Situated in an educationally backward area in the village of Indri in the

Teaching at Sangam

Kangra valley near Sohna, it seeks to provide a good basic education for 5 to 13 year olds within a caring environment, without any divisions or prejudice according to religion or caste. The word *sangam* means "integration". No child is turned away for lack of money; parents are asked to contribute what they can, and the foundation provides the rest. The school seeks to provide "a balance between the material and the spiritual; the rural and the urban; and the aesthetic with utilitarian; the traditional and the modern".

It is easy to underestimate the achievements of Kamla and her staff. The aims of the school seem so commonsensical, so central to any idea of good education that it is hard to imagine that it is revolutionary or extraordinary in any way. But in the context of the school system in India, particularly in rural areas, it *is* extraordinary. Many private schools are set up to make money for their administrators with very little concern for the quality of the education offered. In the state schools teachers are often sent miles from their homes unless they are prepared to bribe an official to avoid such a fate, and often end up bitter and demotivated. A large number of children do not attend school at all. The result is a system that fails the children of India with a colossal wastage of talent. While we were there, the newspapers reported underspending of public schools' budgets, so that even the basic fabric of the buildings is crumbling.

Kamla works with complete dedication, as do her staff, who accept wages about half those in the public sector. We thoroughly enjoyed our two weeks there, teaching English as a double act. We taught the children action songs – "Head and Shoulders, Knees and Toes" – and tried to get them to speak. Their grammar was far better than that of most English schoolchildren, and they had learnt a great deal by rote, but found it very hard to speak or show any initiative.

We found the children delightful: the smallest of them running in late across the field, smart in their blue and white uniforms, each with an over-large satchel on the back, a tiffin tin in the hand. At break we were besieged by groups of children wanting to spend time with us, the girls dragging me off to play badminton in the playground.

At the end of the week several groups of children presented us with beautiful colourful handmade cards, one in an envelope marked "OPEN WITH LOVE". The whole school put on a performance of poetry reading, dance and playlets for "Uncle and Auntie" on the natural stage outside. We sang for them, but were embarrassed to find we only knew one verse of "We Shall Overcome" whereas the children of all ages could sing the whole of it, in English! We were staggered at the keenness and discipline of the children who seemed to attend school not least because they wanted to.

———

Paul and Martin are an Australian and a New Zealander who have lived in India on and off for many years. They are both Quaker attenders, and when we heard of them as isolated Friends, we made an effort to meet them in Chennai, where they now live. Paul and Martin belong to a self-financed community called Jesus Christians, and devote their life to working for the poor. They try to live as much as possible in the way of the first disciples, with no money, no thought for the future. Inspired by the film *Gandhi*, they came over to India some 20 years ago, in the first place to cover over sewers so that a children's playground might be built. They then ran a first aid clinic, and now, with others, devote themselves to creating spiritual books in English with a simplified vocabulary, and selling them on local trains. They had joined the band of vendors that tramp up and down the carriages of many of the trains we had travelled on.

Modest, devoted, models of a Gandhian Christian life.

———

The motto of the multi-faceted charity of ISARA is "dedication, devotion and discipline", and we certainly saw it in evidence among the young staff, living in difficult conditions in most cases far from their homes. Two of the senior staff were Brahmins consecrating their lives to working with untouchables. Unlike the staff of some of the large international NGOs, their pay was negligible; conditions of work basic.

They ate in the office building, and slept there too, on mats on the floor. Their washing facilities consisted of a bucket in the yard; they had little in their lives except work.

We were put up at a government circuit house in Ramagiri, Orissa, opposite their headquarters. It was prestigious and roomy accommodation, though very poorly maintained. There was only one mosquito net, so we had to use it sideways to cover our top halves. No running water, and the one light switch worked all the lights including the one in Vishy's quarters. I did find Indian bathrooms difficult. Most are permanently wet underfoot, often with precipitous steps and bitey insects; only buckets of cold water to clean ourselves and the pan; a hose instead of toilet paper. Stephen rather took to these methods, and when we had an Indian visitor after our return to England, she requested two buckets instead of using the shower.

After a couple of nights we had to leave our quarters to make room for a local MP, and were transferred to "the Tibetan bungalow" in the Tibetan refugee village of Chandragiri some miles away. We were given the room next to the one reserved for the Dalai Lama when he visits, and were allowed into his room, which has incense burning continually in the shrine. The whole place was very spacious, in its own grounds, with a sitting room and hot water. How could we be so lucky? But it poured with rain most of the time we were there, and we had to walk in the pitch dark to a village a mile or so away to eat. The power was off a good deal and both of us got the runs. The Tibetan caretaker, with whom we sadly could not communicate, was a broad-faced friendly man. He stood and watched me write by candlelight, fascinated by our script, and thought nothing of wandering into the bedroom when I was still in bed.

Vishy was trying to raise money for a tribal centre near by, and he felt that its propinquity to the Tibetans would be beneficial; he was most impressed by what they had achieved in the years that they had been there. Hardworking and clear-sighted people, they had acquired a lot of funding and were doing pretty well. Indeed, when we went to visit the Tibetan offices in the village, the young man who greeted us was rather complacent, and indicated a community content to rest on its laurels, even though a number of them were unemployed.

With ISARA we travelled to projects far in the interior of Orissa: to hill tribe villages, where the inhabitants speak their own language and had not seen Westerners before. We were stared at with amazement everywhere we went – dropped jaws at the strange sight of white-skinned people, one with a bald head, the other with very short white hair. Creatures from another planet. The villages were so remote that they could be reached only on the back of a motorbike, so, taking my courage in both hands, I rode pillion, without a crash helmet, sometimes for up to an hour and a half over stone-filled dirt paths, praying that I would not be thrown off. But what sights! We travelled through jungle, with limpid pools on either side, along winding little paths, past isolated houses and villages. Again deep resolve and fear fought within me as I affirmed to myself that *this* was what I had wanted from the entire journey. Here was where I wanted to be.

We were treated as honoured guests, with garlands and ululations. No work. We tried to swallow our disappointment, understanding that our contribution was as an affirmation of the work that was being done by the staff. Also that by visiting the women's self-help groups, we were confirming that the work mattered and the women mattered, in the face of belief to the contrary from the male members of the community.

The houses comprised a bare whitewashed room; there were no facilities for washing or cooking – women cooked on communal fires in the street. Despite UN developmental aid to buy back land from moneylenders, the poverty of the land on the slopes of the hills and the shortage of water meant that it was hard to survive; it was a three-hour walk to market. There were few wells and those that existed were often polluted. The landless were looked after by the rest of the village; some could not even afford rice, but ate a poor substitute.

We visited "innovative" schools, night schools for children from 6 to 14 who work during the day. With volunteer teachers from their own community, they learn with slates and by the light of lanterns

– only two for a class of 25. I asked what made the innovative schools innovative, apart from the fact that they took place at night. Not the teaching methods, it appeared, but the content which was related to the children's daily lives, the geography of the region and so on. All very practical, but pedestrian: there was little to liberate their imaginations and creative abilities.

The women in one village seemed passive, almost cowed, and Stephen and I came separately to the conclusion that domestic violence was at the root of it. The ISARA workers confirmed that abuse was prevalent in the villages; they hoped that once the women's groups gained strength, they would increasingly feel able to fight abuse on a collective basis. In general, though, they were certainly stronger than the Muslim women I had met in Bangladesh a few years before. Here, when asked if the men minded them having the money, the secretary of one group said, "It's our money. They had all the say before; now it's us."

On the whole the tribal people did not look much different from other Indians though I gathered that the remote villages we went to had only mixed with other villages for a couple of generations, and still kept local customs. I would have liked to learn more about the different tribes, but there was an uncomfortable vagueness about it all at ISARA, as well as a language barrier. Uriya is the local language, but few of the tribal people spoke it.

At night we chatted with the young ISARA staff, persuading them to allow us to eat with them off banana leaves on the floor. One of them had written a report on HIV/AIDS, which was prevalent in the region. I was surprised that in a culture which is so family-oriented and in which promiscuity is rare HIV should be a problem. Apparently men have to go far afield to find work, get lonely, have contact with sex workers, and return home once a year, infecting their wives. Sufferers become untouchable. We heard of a sick 17-year-old boy, who was put in a cattle shed outside the village, not even given food by his mother.

The other project that ISARA and Vishy took us to was in a remote coastal area devastated by a cyclone a year or so before. It was in a village of 1,400 people, isolated from their neighbours by being Teluga speakers, and driven from their previous village for opposing the pushing of liquor by their higher caste neighbours. ISARA were implementing a programme of building new houses, also advising and training 11 women's self-help groups. Though there was no outside money to give them, the women themselves were giving out loans from their savings. We were moved by their determination and the altruism of the villagers as a whole. It was the village that decided who would get the new houses, a decision made on the basis of greatest need. We were followed everywhere by a huge procession and given the most beautiful garlands. The women sang; I sang "Blow the Wind Southerly", and a little disabled boy in an immaculate white shirt was carried to the front of the crowd and sang to us in a high pure treble. He was their star. I was always the only woman among the visitors on these occasions and it was to me that the women came, asking for help. Being treated like the Queen, partly because of my age, didn't make me feel any less helpless.

Also from a tribal background was the head of the next NGO that we visited with Vishy. Mr Banja had had the good fortune to be educated at a Ramakrishna mission, and felt a need to improve the lot of his own people, and of scheduled caste people in the area of West Bengal where he lives. After nearly fifty years he still feels part of that excluded community and adheres to his old practices, sleeping, as he has always done, on the floor. Mr Banja is a plump and cheerful elderly man who talks with enthusiasm, particularly about Bakcha, the NGO that he started up from scratch in 1955. All on one site, a huge compound comprises paddy fields, a high school, a primary school and hostels for boys and girls. When international aid arrived after the cyclone, he collected the sacks and, by selling them, raised enough money to build the fabric of a new school. The doors and windows are yet to come.

The playing field of the school is used by the local villagers, and the new water supply from a tube well 600 foot deep, funded by the Japanese, benefits the local village too. The impact of the project has reached every family in the community.

All the children there are destitute or scheduled (untouchable) caste. As the young women grew up, Mr Banja realised that their chances of marriage were poor, and he started a training programme in weaving and mat-making. I managed to talk to a few of them in limited Bangla and discovered that each mat took two days to make, for which they received R10 (about 12p). I encouraged the staff to think about self-employment from which the women would gain much more.

Midnapore is on the borders of West Bengal and Orissa, and often misses out on the relief given to either. Mr Banja has a considerable problem with the local Communist council or *punchyat*, who are jealous of his success. It is through them that the government money that he is given comes, and they try every possible ploy to deny it to him. Even when he gets it, it is always in arrears, and he is left fumbling for enough money to buy food for the children. Like Vishy, he has been threatened several times, once with a gun in front of the children. He will not give in to protection rackets or submit to corruption. When we gave him a donation for the school to cover the expenses of putting us up on site, he hastily gave the money to the treasurer. He did not want to get involved in the handling of any finances.

Prayer in action is love. Love in action is service.
Mother Teresa

Birbati is the eight-year-old daughter of a prostitute, conceived in the line of her mother's work. She has had polio and also has learning difficulties, and in the mid-1990s was living with a number of other street children on Howrah station, Kolkata. The children spoke English, and received a broad general education from the backpackers passing through, and from the television which blasts over the station.

Our friend, Margaret, who was then working in Kolkata, came through Howrah station every day, and was appalled by the filthy state of these children. There was on platform no. 1 a water pump that had been installed by the British in the days of the Raj, and which was used by many of the people on the station. She suggested to some of the children that they might like to have a wash, but the children explained that, being small, they could not break into the hierarchy that jealously guarded the pump. Margaret and a friend, however, muscled in, and to the delight of the children, gave them a wash. The women saw this as a one-off effort, but the children accosted them every time they came through the station to do it again. Now that the precedent had been set, they managed to persuade the children and their mothers to do it themselves, and a new routine was set up.

In 1992 Margaret and some friends set up a charity called TRACKS, which included a station school at Howrah. The children were taught on platform 8, and the school books and charts were stored in trunks in the only safe place on the station: the shrine of the elephant god, Ganesh. As a result of the school, many of the mothers approached Margaret and her friends and asked them to help with their children, look after them, even take them away. Margaret started up a mother and child project to try to educate the women in child care, but then came across Birbati, then aged about six months, whose mother was drug-addicted and unable to look after her. When the mother was run over by a train, Margaret and a friend actually carried her to the Sisters of Mercy in Kolkata, who were unable to take her in. They finally found her a place at Nirmal Hirady (the Home for the Dying) by pretending that the sisters had sent them. Meanwhile, Margaret had taken baby Birbati and placed her in the residential home for severely disabled children that she had helped start up. Some years later, when the school fell into difficulties, Birbati was rescued and taken to Mr Banja's school – the first disabled child at Bakcha. And there she thrives as does TRACKS, now run entirely by local people.

———

For the last two weeks of our time in India, we were in a project near Dharamsala. The overnight bus from Delhi was crowded, and the temperature dropped as the bus climbed into the foothills of the

Nuns celebrating Tibetan New Year

Himalayas. These buses stopped every few hours for eating stops – usually around midnight and four in the morning. This bus felt like a foreign country. It was full of Tibetans, for we were heading for the main community of Tibetans in India, and their New Year, not coincidentally at the same time as the Chinese one, in February, was nearly upon us.

A few days later we got up before dawn to witness the New Year celebrations, in the village of McLeodganj, up above the snow line and freezing cold in the early morning. Though his residence was near by, the Dalai Lama himself did not attend, as he was recuperating from illness. The ceremony was watched by a crowd of Tibetans, and by a number of tourists. Monks with vivid orange headgear like mohican haircuts sat on the ground blowing six-foot-long bass trumpets and chanting in a low rumble, accompanied by some of the elderly Tibetans in the crowd. It was a touching affirmation of their identity but was not aimed at entertaining an audience.

The branch of Hinduism that runs from Ramakrishna through Vivekananda, Ramana and Aurobindo is alive and kicking in the magnificent person of Kshama Metre and the charity she runs near Dharamsala. It is called the Chinmaya Tapovan Trust (CTT) and is one of some 250 missions, schools and old age homes founded in 25 countries by her guru, Swami Chinmayananda ("ananda" means "blessed"). Guru Dev, as he is familiarly known, laid considerable emphasis on work as worship, an ethos that lives on throughout this centre where hundreds of young people work often seven days a week and late into the night either as volunteers or for very little money out in the field with the more disadvantaged of their community. The greeting at CTT was "Hare Om" (the word of God); the day started with collective worship, as it did at each of the projects, and the garlanded photo and influence of Guru Dev was always to the fore.

The programmes in the rural areas of Kangra District involve 370 villages, and include primary health care services, women's self-help groups, playgroups, literacy projects, adolescent girls' and boys' groups, sanitation, income generation and work with disabilities and alcohol abuse. The work affects several thousand villagers every year. Kshama, or Dr Didi as she is known, is a living example of all this NGO stands for. A large, statuesque woman with dark penetrating eyes, my first memory of her is as we were sitting in front of her in her study, awaiting instructions. A young woman came in with a tiny baby, a few days old. Kshama picked it up, examined it tenderly but dispassionately, said a few words to the mother and carried on with the rest of her business. She is a paediatrician by training and practises on the hop, as she runs the centre.

At last Stephen and I were put to work. No nonsense here. As soon as we arrived, Kshama asked us to write a little about ourselves so that she could decide which project would be suitable. I, full of confidence that at last my knowledge of microcredit could be used, was crestfallen when she said matter-of-factly that my Hindi wasn't good enough. We had taken some lessons in Delhi, but then had been in states where the languages were Malalayam, Telugu, Tamil, Uriya – no chance to

Kshama preparing for a village celebration

practise Hindi. India has 15 official languages – all on the banknotes. No wonder the use of English is so widespread among educated people. But here we were working with people with little or no education – indeed, even in this Hindi area, many only spoke village languages.

Stephen was asked to participate in a new project of resource management, and was in seventh heaven wandering round the small villages in the mountains, looking at the woods, water and grass and coming up with ideas of how to make the most of them.

Kshama asked me to teach English to her assistant, Rajiv, who needed to improve his written English in order to take dictation from her. She also offered me either adult literacy – "But I can't read Hindi!" "No, but you could learn alongside them" – or help with the kinder-gartens (*bhalwaris*) that they had set up in villages where there were no other schools. There were dozens of *bhalwaris*, but the two to which Kshama suggested I went were in the slums. I agreed with alacrity.

Then followed two of the most fascinating, if exhausting, weeks of my life. I had done some work with homeless people in London, and as I got off the bone-shaker bus at the first slum, my feeling was the same. When I joined the young local teacher in wandering through the black plastic "growing frame" tents calling, "School, school, *jaldi, jaldi*," I felt a swelling of my heart, a lump in my throat and the conviction that these were "my" people. I am particularly drawn to excluded people, and this community, from another state – Rajasthan – speaking another language and living for 25 years on the edge of the town and of accepted life in this part of India, were indeed excluded.

The "schools" were basic: in one case a scruffy little concrete hut at the back of a graffiti-strewn bus shelter type of building, reached by picking our way across broken glass and human excrement; in the other a black plastic tent like their homes; both dark with the door shut, deafening when it rained. And it was cold: we were just below the snow line, and it was winter. No light or heat. Fifteen children and three of us "teachers" sat on mats on the ground.

The children were dirty little urchins with, in most cases, only one set of clothes, ranging in age from six months to about ten years old. There was a pump near by, but perhaps they were excluded from using it. Nearly all were married, even the two- or three-year-olds,

Slum bhalwari

and one of the big boys, who was very bright and should have been at school, was on drugs, as were all his family. There were a teacher and assistant for each school, with not much education and inherited methods of teaching, by rote, and with too much use of the stick. I tried to liven the mornings up with animal noises, songs and games – generally playing the fool. I loved it. At the end of some sessions I took them outside for Grandmother's Footsteps, Hokey Cokey and Ring a Ring o' Roses. There was great excitement and much laughter.

On one occasion I took some rough paper and got them to draw. They had never drawn freehand before, only coloured in shapes stencilled by the teachers. We communicated in what the teacher referred to as "tutti frutti" English or in my case "tutti frutti" Hindi. I made them draw big, using the whole page, and sharing the crayons – taking only one at a time. I then asked the teacher to put their names on, so that they could begin to recognise them, and then they took the pictures home. Unheard of!

There was a great sense of being able to make a difference: Kshama had the power to make things happen. When I reported back

Slum bhalwari

and told her of some of my misgivings, she said immediately that she would send a health visitor to train the mothers in hygiene, and asked me to hold a workshop with all the teachers, summoning them all to gather a couple of days later.

I had never held a workshop or done role play, but thoroughly enjoyed the challenge. An Kush, one of a pair of brother volunteers from Mumbai, interpreted for me, and we asked the teachers to be children for the day, assigning roles such as bully, shy child, baby, mothering girl, naughty child etc. We took the role of teacher, first disciplinarian (such as I had seen in one place) then laissez-faire. The "children" thoroughly enjoyed themselves, really letting their hair down for once. As one woman assigned the "naughty" role emptied a jar full of crayons on to the floor with evident satisfaction, I reflected that she had probably not been allowed to have such fun even as a child. In the afternoon we explored more reasonable ways of dealing with their charges, with all those different age groups, and asked them to share their difficulties.

I was anxious not to lose the opportunity of some interaction in the field of microcredit. Kshama agreed that I might hold a workshop for about fifty of the workers, also interpreted by An Kush. The session took the form of a sharing of information, since there was little that I could teach these young women. They were staggered that anyone in such a rich country as Britain should need microcredit. They could not imagine that we had poverty. I further shocked them by telling them of some of our social problems: broken families, isolated single mothers, asylum seekers, the benefit trap etc. I think they got a pretty negative view of Western society. They were surprised to hear that savings played no part in our scheme, that in Britain, as in other developed countries, it simply is not legal to lend from savings (except for Credit Unions).

"So how do you make it work, then? Why would the women feel a loyalty to the organisation?"

Stephen and I stayed at the connected ashram down the road, paying for our keep. It was a five-minute walk, and we were seriously warned not to go along the road alone at night, as leopards came down from the hills after dark. There had been reports of attacks on people, since food for the animals, as for the people, was scarce. Stephen, frustrated, as I was, by not having seen many wild animals on our travels, walked along the road at twilight calling "pussy, pussy"!

Apart from the work, we gained hugely from living in such a Spirit-led organisation; in having the opportunity when time allowed to discuss faith matters with, for instance, An Kush. He and his brother had volunteered for CTT for six months, both highly educated skilled young men, as well as people who live their faith. An Kush was a devout Hindu who gave a lot of credence to miracles and other religious phenomena. He told stories of holy men who had been protected, even from the rain, and his views are backed up by many of the sages:

> There have been cases where because one man with a strong destiny, a developed consciousness, has been in a ship, that ship has escaped disaster though it should normally have sunk. But these are complicated subjects. So many factors are involved – the choice of the soul, the destiny of the person, the collective destiny of the people who are already there, and God's intentions.
>
> M. P. Pandit, *Spiritual Life*, p.225.

It was on such subjects that I ceased to be at ease with Hindu beliefs. For me karma and reincarnation were stumbling blocks.

It was primarily Kshama herself who inspired us, and I took every opportunity both to tell her about what I was doing, and also to discuss with her matters of theology: meditation, contemplation, and the many paths to a change of consciousness.

We spent three months in India and, by the time we left, felt acclimatised. It was hard to leave. India and its spiritual consciousness seems to seep into the bones; one absorbs a different way of seeing, of experiencing the world. It has something to do with the gentleness and forbearance of Indian people. Despite appalling conditions, people simply live their lives and take the longer view, an attitude that is powerfully influential. People said we would want to go back to India; we do and we will.

No Man's Land

*A*lthough it meant going "backwards" in our westerly progress round the world, to catch our Singapore Airlines plane to Beijing we had to go to Singapore.

The culture shock was almost physical. We had left the cold of North India, and arrived in a steamy, hot and humid city. The streets were immaculately clean; the flat we stayed in was part of a luxury block with designer swimming pool; the city was one vast shopping mall. I was not there long enough to discover how poorer people lived on the underbelly of such a materialist society; I know that our host Anne, a splendid Quaker teacher, felt very uneasy with the life she had been plunged into. Certainly the flat, isolated from her neighbours, would not have been her choice.

On the bus going to one of the main tourist attractions, the "Night Safari", was a young American family. The little boy did not like the seat he was in and threw a tantrum until he was moved to one next to a window. Fresh from India, I was staggered at the difference in behaviour. Never, in India, did we see a child behave like that. With all the deprivation and poverty, we hardly heard a child cry. The contrast between children in Singapore, confident and affluent, in restaurants and shops, and the slum children I had been working with was so great. Just the same in capacity, yet worlds apart in what they can expect from life, and what they get.

We did arrange a Meeting for Worship in Singapore, with Anne, another American teacher called Mark, a visiting English Quaker and two elderly Chinese sisters, in their lovely flat. For them it was a rare experience. For me it was an oasis in an alien land. When I said to Mark, "I don't like tourists or shopping," he said, "You've come to the wrong place."

———

We hadn't wanted to go to China either. I had spent three weeks there 15 years before on a "business" trip, and hadn't liked it. Indeed, it had made me wonder whether I was tired of travel. Since then, everything that friends had told me of recent changes – the high rise flats, the increasing consumerism – had done nothing to make me want to go there again.

But, to catch the Trans-Siberian Express, it was to Beijing that we had to go. And it was different this time. High rise, certainly, and, astoundingly, there were young men walking through the streets, carrying Pierre Cardin bags. There were fewer bikes and more cars – it felt a city transformed. But this time we were staying with friends of friends – a delightful Chinese intellectual family, and in one of the few remaining old quarters. So, against expectation, I enjoyed it, and wished we had been staying longer.

The old man of the family, Yang Xianyi, was a renowned scholar – indeed, our taxi driver recognised him, as he had been on TV the previous week. He and his English wife, Gladys, who died a couple of years before, had worked for the Foreign Languages Press and as a result, were highly suspect during the Cultural Revolution. They were both sent to prison for four years – Gladys in solitary confinement. Xianyi, an imperturbable, Oxford-educated Confucian, talked entertainingly about his time in prison as he sat with us, chain-smoking and drinking a viciously strong Chinese liquor. He had met thieves and murderers – "Such interesting men" – and taught them English songs. The picture of Chinese criminals singing "Drink to Me Only With Thine Eyes" was quite surreal.

Xianyi's daughter Yang Zhi was our hostess. She and her Canadian husband, David, were academics who now ran their own cuttings agency. She was a Marxist, and frank, as was the rest of the family, about the corruption that was an everyday occurrence in their lives. To build their house they had had to bribe large numbers of organisations, and to pursue a court case against a former employee they had had to pay for the police officers to spend an evening in a gambling club. They agreed that life had been difficult and unpredictable – Yang Zhi had been sent into the countryside as a young woman and had quite enjoyed it – but they did not feel another Cultural Revolution would turn their lives upside down.

"There's no one to lead it," Yang Zhi said. "The young are only interested in shopping."

It was a wonderful stay. We slotted into their family life with ease. Feeling guilty at being given their bed, especially when an older friend turned up from England to stay, we suggested moving to a hotel. It was the only occasion on which David grew fierce. "Certainly not. We won't hear of it."

The night before we left, an extraordinary thing happened. We were talking after supper about the meaning of surnames and Stephen untypically mentioned that of his birth father, whom he had never known. All he knew was that his father had been a prominent member of the British Communist Party, and had been wounded in the Spanish Civil War. Yang Xianyi stared ruminatively at the ceiling and blew out some smoke.

"I knew a man of that name," he said. There was silence in the room; a stillness as it became apparent that this old man, whom we had only met by the slimmest of chances, had known Stephen's father. It turned out that the Englishman had come out to China after the revolution as a translator for the Chinese Communist Party. He had developed throat cancer and had been sent to Moscow to be cured. He had died out there, and his body had been brought back to Beijing to be buried in a hero's grave. There was no time for us to visit it, but Stephen spoke on the phone to a former friend of his father's in Beijing and now has names to contact in England. His father, it seems, was a man of principle, highly thought of by many. It was a powerful moment for us all.

Although we were only there for a week, we learnt a different perspective in China. One evening, as drink loosened the tongues of our host and an outspoken resident Australian guest, they spoke forcibly of the distorted views of the West, and of the United States in particular. Although it was obvious that they were deliberately provocative in some of what they said, for instance about the Taliban protecting women, it was clear that their take on world affairs was utterly different from our own. It reminded us that our newspapers too have their own slant; it is not only the Americans who are insular; not only the Communist papers that propagate propaganda. It confirmed me in my view that news is an artificial and subjective concept; what it is seen to consist in depends on the view of the editor and the owner of the paper or broadcasting station concerned.

CHAPTER 13

The Last Pristine Land

The Creator of the world is the owner of it

John Woolman

*I*magine a country without fences or boundaries, in which all land is in common ownership. Vast expanses of space uncluttered by trees, rocks or any recognisable feature, except clusters of wild ponies and camels, and gazelles that streak across the horizon in terror at the sound of a vehicle. Imagine a country with temperatures down to –40°c in the winter and up to +40°c in the summer. A nomadic population: hardy but hospitable, and one of the worst diets in the world.

That's Mongolia, and we were there in March.

We were there because Martha, one of my former writer clients, lives there for part of the year. The last time I saw her was 15 years ago, when I visited her in Seattle. She had just returned from her first trip to Mongolia and had rung her husband, John, to say: "This is the last pristine country on earth. We must live here." A tiny vibrant American woman with startling blue eyes, Martha is a specialist on Chinese affairs. She helped set up a publishing programme for the Soros Foundation in Mongolia, and also set up a women's weavers' co-operative with her own money, as the aid was not getting through. Martha was one of the central characters in my concept of this journey and, although I sadly did not see her, we made contact. In reply to an email from me describing what I was looking for in Mongolia, she offered a generous affirmation of my way of life that echoed my powerful recognition of hers.

Stephen and I had taken the Trans-Mongolian train from Beijing: the first stage of the legendary Trans-Siberian Express. Many people confuse the Trans-Siberian Express with the Orient Express. The TSE, however, is not a luxury tourist train, but a workaday means of transport for local traders and business people. In second class it is certainly comfortable, with linen provided, and a boiler with constant hot water at the end of each carriage. Each carriage has a *provodnitsa* or concierge. We had been warned about the fierceness, particularly of some of the Russian ones, but actually they looked after us like mother hens. Especially Stephen, who went out jogging at every stop. And it's easy to miss the train. Unlike the trains in India which leave with plenty of warning toots and move slowly out of the station with plenty of time to finish a conversation and board it, a Russian train leaves speedily and silently. It can be gone before you notice it is moving.

The other reason it's easy to miss is that there are several different time zones in action at once. One passes through five time zones on the six-day trip, but the train departures are all according to Moscow time, which, as one hasn't reached it yet going from East to West, can be confusing – especially as the restaurant car and lights out times are on local time.

At the China/Mongolia border, we were surprised to see Mongolians buying large quantities of eggs, tomatoes and other vegetables to take home. As we found later, vegetables are hard to come by in the harsh Mongolian climate, and much cheaper over the border. At our first stop in the snow-dotted steppes, early on a chilly morning, a clutch of eager high-cheeked Mongolian salespeople wrapped in coats, hats, scarves and boots met us with thermoses full of dumplings and bottles of *airag* (fermented mares' milk). I had no Mongolian money, but a young woman from further up the carriage insisted on treating me: "Welcome to Mongolia!" The pork dumplings made a greasy but delicious breakfast for the four of us in our compartment.

Mongolia has recovered its independence after years of subjugation first by the Chinese, then by the Soviet Union. The present country, at over one and a half million square kilometres three times the size of France, used to be double that – part has now been swallowed up into Siberia, Russia, and Inner Mongolia is now part of China. When the USSR collapsed, Mongolia became free, but at a price. In the early 1990s inflation rose to 300%; the country lost the equivalent of

50% of its net expenditure; and urban unemployment shot up. People reverted to traditional ways of herding and traditional forms of transport. Despite free education, economic pressure has meant that the high literacy rate is falling and nearly a million people live below the poverty line.

Ulaanbaatar, the capital of Mongolia, is an unattractive scruffy town with patchy architecture, much of it Soviet, including the apartment block in which our guest house was situated. Places do not have addresses but are just described as near something else, so it was easy to get lost, though some knowledge of Russian meant that I could at least read the Cyrillic script. Though it's a poor country, some people have money, as evidenced by some smart cars and a few people wearing fur coats. Most, though, still dress in the traditional *del*, a full-length woollen coat/dress worn by men and women, and tied with a bright sash. It looks very dashing if worn by a man with traditional shoes with curled toes and the essential hat.

Stephen was pickpocketed twice in Ulaanbaatar: once as he got off the train, and the second time coming out of the supermarket. I felt an atmosphere of menace in the town that I had not felt since Guatemala City, and wasn't happy wandering around, especially at night. I felt the usual guilt and indecision about giving to beggars – nearly all children – one of whom hit me when I refused to give. There are 3,000 children living in the sewers: street children who have to go underground to survive the extreme temperatures. We felt rather helpless with this knowledge, but Stephen tracked down an orphanage to which he gave a donation of $30. He couldn't understand why they were quite so grateful, but discovered the reason when he heard from a high school teacher that she earned $50 a month. The orphanage was so overwhelmed by the gift that they insisted on putting the news on local radio.

Ulaanbaatar is the coldest capital in the world, and it was cold even in March: -20°c at night and about -5°c during the day. It was wonderful crisp, dry weather, humidity nil, with bright blue skies which made sunglasses imperative. It was often quite windy too, penetrating all but the most efficient layers of clothing. My lovely Bolivian jacket at last came into its own, after months of carrying it round hot countries, as did the silk long johns that I had bought from Marks & Spencer: light, squashable and warm. With the padded trousers, fleecy cardigan and hat with ear flaps bought in China, plus a hand-knitted scarf from Tibet, I was snug even in the worst of the weather.

Silence demands space, space in the whole structure of consciousness . . . When there is silence, there is immense, timeless space; then only is there a possibility of coming upon that which is the eternal, sacred.

J. Krishnamurti, *The Wholeness of Life*

My instinct, as always, was to get out of the town, and we soon found a van and driver to take us to the Gobi desert, and two young Danish women, Maria and Agneta, to share the costs. Six days in the desert – at last. We stocked up with food at the State Department Store, an old-fashioned large building with dusty windows. We were told that we would be staying in *gers* (traditional felt tents) and supper and breakfast would be provided. We bought provisions for lunches: eggs which I hardboiled, fruit, cheese, bread, jam, some pasta, tea, and fuel for the little stove that came with the van. Choice was limited and, for once, the ubiquitous Coke or Pepsi was not available. We fortunately bought plenty of food, as we ended up feeding Gera, the driver, even though we had been told that he would supply his own.

Gera was magnificent. He did not speak English, but we managed to communicate using my phrase book and the universal language of gesture. A few miles out of UB the road petered out, leaving him reliant on distant peaks to guide him, plus the occasional tracks made by other vehicles. In general the land was brown and gritty. Miles of empty space and vast horizons. I love the desert: in such landscapes my soul expands. I was frustrated by the fact that there were few opportunities to walk. With a vehicle and fellow passengers, it was hard to abscond. I did early one morning climb a hill near the *ger* in which we had been staying and found a shamanistic *ovoo* or cairn with the head of a mountain goat with curved horns as an offering. I sat quietly for ten minutes or so, drinking in the space, the peace, the landscape – what I had come for.

And sometimes during the hours of driving I persuaded the others to go ahead for a few miles and brew up while I walked on. Outside I jumped up and down, danced for joy. I wanted to spend hours, days just walking in the wilderness into the immeasurable distance. Because I could see the van, a dot on the horizon, I sometimes turned and walked backwards to give myself the illusion of solitude. I wanted to be alone.

In few places does the Gobi conform to the general idea of desert landscape. The Mongolians count 33 types of desert, and some of it has enough grass for livestock to graze, but the Khongoryn Els in the extreme south of the Gobi is all that one could wish for: a huge range of sand dunes, 12km wide by about 100km long and 800 metres high. We reached them over a frozen river, worrying whether the van would crack the ice. They were wonderful high dunes, reminiscent of Egypt

Khongoryn Els, Gobi Desert

– the sensuous curves ending in a razor edge; the wave-like patterns on the sand; the dramatic shadows. I climbed up and lay on the untouched golden sand. Then the glorious late evening sun touched the whiskery plants and small shrubs and imbued them with a glow that reminded me of the south of France after harvest – golden, deceptively fertile-looking.

The Gobi is, however, different from the Egyptian Western Desert in the richness of its animal inhabitants: dumpy wild horses, recognisable from afar by their plodding walk, heads down; herds of mixed sheep and goats, usually without human guardians; gazelles; and stately bearded two-humped Bactrian camels, much shorter and fluffier than their haughty brothers. One day we saw a few of them drinking at a water hole and as Stephen and Gera pushed the bar to pump water for them, others plodded up from far and wide. Sometimes we saw vultures, and there was a lot for them to feed on. Evidence of the harshness of the climate was everywhere – bones of horses and sheep, sometimes picked clean, sometimes still intact.

And at night we stayed with local people in *gers*, large circular tents with a parasol structure, rising to a point in the middle, with a hole for the chimney of the central stove. The arrangement of *gers* is pretty standard. The master bed is at the back of the *ger*, others to right and left, with an altar area to the right of the main bed with shrine and candle and some precious possessions. If the owners are not Buddhist, the altar will consist mainly of family photos. The cooking and eating area (we sat on little stools) is in the centre; near the entrance is stored a container of precious water where people wash their hands and face, usually taking the water into the mouth and squirting it on to their hands to wash.

We saw no evidence of any other washing, or indeed undressing, though none of the Mongolians we met smelt. I felt extremely uncomfortable after six days of not washing, though I did on one occasion heat some water in the van and walk off into the distance to wash the crucial bits. There is no privacy inside the *ger* or out. Lavatorial activities take place round the back of the *ger* or, when

Mongolian hosts

travelling, behind the van, men and women taking it in turns. This is an outdoor culture, and a cold one. Our water and food in the van were frozen – waterlogged bananas, cucumbers and tomatoes a good lesson in what not to bring. Even at midday, after hours of sun, the water I washed my face in had ice in it.

On arrival at a *ger*, the customary call is not of "hello" but "*Nokhoi Khor*" ("hold the dog"). Dogs are fierce here, sometimes rabid, and to be taken seriously. Once inside, we were always offered tea, made by heating a vast bowlful of water on the stove, a little milk and salt added, and a sprinkling of tea dust. We got quite used to this salty drink; any hot drink is welcome. With it is offered a bowl of bread so hard it is impossible to break without dunking it in the tea, and sometimes interspersed for the unwary with similar-looking rocks of inedible strong cheese. Meals are invariably of old mutton, brought in, frozen, from the outside, hacked into pieces and boiled up with doughy noodles. Sometimes a skilful hostess made more out of the same basic ingredients, but the smell of old mutton was ubiquitous.

Etiquette, as our guide book informed us, is complex. Don't step on the threshold, don't touch someone's hat, don't point your feet at anyone. Don't show your wrists, spill milk or write in red ink. On entering, walk clockwise round to the left, sitting towards the back in the area reserved for guests. Everything is given and received with both hands, or the right one, supported by the left. There are rituals surrounding the offering of snuff or vodka, even if the owner is too poor for the ornate bottle actually to contain anything. Never throw anything on the fire. Fire is sacred; on one occasion, a Mongolian friend we were travelling with brought some food from Ulaanbaatar specifically to offer to the fire, as his home in the capital had no open fire.

On no occasion did we stay in tourist *ger* camps, but it soon became clear that we were being guided to *gers* which were used to receiving visitors, basic accommodation but almost like bed-and-breakfast establishments, and there was a similar impersonal attitude, a professionalism that spoilt the experience of meeting local people. One night, we stayed with a family who, very strangely, departed for the night, leaving their home to the five of us (Maria, Agneta, Stephen, Gera and myself). After we had settled down, Stephen needed to have a pee and headed off with his torch to the tin hut that served the group of local *gers*. A lavatory was a rarity and we welcomed the shelter from the wind, even if one side was open to the elements, and inside merely two slippery planks with a gap over a hole. He was gone a long while and I began to wonder, then heard him calling, from way off: "Hello, hello" and a cacophony of dogs barking. His torch had failed, he had lost his bearings in the dark, and had spent the last half hour wandering around. There was no way of locating my coat, hat, scarf or boots in the dark, so I made my way over sleeping bodies to the flap of the door, lit a candle and went out in my bare feet, calling to him. The candle of course blew out, but we did in the end find our way in.

We slept well, I in one bed, the two girls in the other, and Gera and Stephen on the floor, uninterrupted save for an extraordinary invasion by three men who came in the middle of the night. Two sat on the girls' bed, and the third ceremoniously lit a candle and looked round at us. Gera raised himself on one elbow and exchanged a few

The tin hut lavatory

sleepy words with them, but no one got up. I kept waiting for someone to say, "What the hell are you doing here?" I expected more drama, but reality is so often tamer than the expectation. The men finally left, and we heard the roar of a motor bike fade into the distance. They could have been officials of some sort; equally they could have murdered us in our beds. Unable to ask Gera the meaning of this night visitation, we never discovered the reason for it. We did hear afterwards however that it used to be quite common for strangers to turn up in the middle of the night and help themselves to whatever they needed. Life is tough and travellers need shelter. Not only is there no private land in Mongolia; there is very little concept of privacy or ownership. Possessions are few and, except for animals, they are contained within the *ger*. Life is semi-nomadic, attachment slight: the very archetype of simplicity.

We all made it clear to Gera that we preferred staying in ordinary *gers*, and he responded. It was much harder going in that the owners were not used to receiving visitors: stoves went out early so that we could not get warm at night, even fully dressed, in sleeping bags and under layers of sheepskins; the food, always difficult, was even more basic, but the experience was much more rewarding. We did in fact always stay with better-off people – others simply would not have had the wherewithal to host an extra five people. Gera could tell from the number of cattle or sheep that were corralled outside the *ger* whether it would be an appropriate place to stay. The poorer people had none. As it was, a member of the household was usually sent out to fetch something from a shop or a neighbour, and went off on a horse or, increasingly likely in modern-day Mongolia, on a motor bike. We usually slept on the floor, feet to the door, or sometimes, as oldies, Stephen and I were offered a bed, and were always tucked in before the family went to bed – a very strange experience, especially as I was usually trying to change some clothing under the blankets as they did so.

We always paid for our one-night stays, whether expected or not. Stephen argues that staying free with people much poorer than ourselves is immoral. I agree but also realise that paying for something that has been free for hundreds of years is undermining a traditional culture. Mongolia is in a transitional era and free hospitality, so much a feature of *ger* culture, will probably disappear in the next ten years, as it has in other countries. The age-old tradition of giving presents is also under threat. Do we pay and give presents too?

Wednesday. Snow storm! Yesterday we drove through a blizzard, Gera manoeuvring his way on disappearing tracks and in near-nil visibility. Peeing in a blizzard, side by side with Agneta in the shelter of the side of the van was quite an experience! We have all got used to peeing in the open, men and women round different sides of the van – men peeing away from the wind, women into it – an important orientation!

When we finally found a group of gers, they turned us away – G. always goes in first to negotiate. Extraordinary to reject us in such terrible conditions. Eventually we came to a small town and drove around asking. We were welcomed into a larger ger than usual by an extended family – mother, who turned out to be a maths teacher and was very modern, trim and sexy; father, big, handsome and traditional in his del; assorted

The Gobi: stuck in the snow

children about ten years old who came and went; grandmother, who visited for a while; and the mother's elder sister who was 9 months pregnant. Extraordinary to welcome 6 of us (we now had a young man in tow from the previous night, who was travelling to UB).

It was the best night of our trip – we played cards and "bones" with the ankle bones of sheep, and sang – all very warm and companionable. S and I finally shared a (small) double bed and were cosy and friendly in a tangle of unzipped sleeping bags and blankets. The other bed was shared by husband, wife and sister-in-law (she sleeping the other way round from the other two!). Good dumplings in a stew last night and rice pudding with lumps of sour cheese dissolved in it this morning. I liked it but the girls gagged.

The drive today, on paper relatively short, was appallingly difficult. Tracks had disappeared and after an hour's driving we plunged into a snowdrift about 3ft deep. The young man eventually dug us out, then the engine failed. We were beginning to have doubts about reaching UB tonight (for M's and A's train to Beijing tomorrow) but G finally got it going. We then came across the only other vehicle we had seen for three days: a stranded jeep whose occupants had spent the night in it. We gave them the last of our

bread and hard-boiled eggs and then towed it for a while. Then G managed
to get their engine going and we started off again and finally reached UB
about 5 p.m., badly in need of a rest and a wash.

What an expedition! And what an opportunity to witness a unique
way of life that challenges our own.

———

In the Gobi we had visited Bayanzag, the "Flaming Cliffs", hard to
find without an experienced driver, and famous for the discovery
of numerous dinosaur bones and eggs now forming part of the
renowned collection in the Natural History Museum in Ulaanbaatar.
So we thought we should go to see them. It is an extraordinary gallery
of the remains of vast dinosaurs, up to 70 million years old, and their
eggs. There were dozens of extinct animals of all sorts, including the
complete skeleton of a meat-eating tarbosaurus of huge proportions,
15 metres high and four to five tons in weight. Also the jaws of another
even bigger. Magnificent but terrifying.

But in all the other galleries, there were hundreds of stuffed
animals, from a mongoose to a moose: a large stately animal taller
than a man. Vast and small birds with outstretched wings: parrots,
humming birds, water birds and vultures. Most impressive of all,
a king eagle. It was impressive – and monstrous. Animals of all
shapes and sizes had been shot for display. Shot carefully so that the
appearance would not be marred by a visible bullet hole. Killed, stuffed
and moulded into a form as lifelike as possible – except that the eyes
are dead, the spirit, that which links the animal world to us as living
creatures, is gone, their poses a hideous mockery of their living form.
In a world that has begun to reject animals jumping through hoops
or imprisoned in small cages, why do we not rebel at this unnecessary
killing? In a land of such freedom, it seemed doubly shocking.

I was not happy at spending five whole days in Ulaanbaatar
until our train left, but I met two Mongolians who made the wait
worthwhile.

Tsog had worked with my friend Martha at the Soros Foundation, and was starting up an English-language college. A big handsome man, he took us under his wing and, in the mistaken belief that we were qualified English teachers, showed us round the college. He heard of my interest in community development and insisted on taking me round a family centre that he supports. We went down into a basement rather reminiscent of some of the homeless shelters in London, and talked to some of the staff who help 33 poor families to learn carpentry, handicrafts and social skills. Tsog felt that microcredit might be appropriate for some of the women at this centre, but he particularly wanted me to visit a women's organisation that a friend of his was involved with.

Mrs Nadmid, the executive director of the feminist organisation LEOS, was the second Mongolian who made an impact on me. She had a patrician presence, and an exquisite face that reminded me of a Japanese painting. She did not speak English, so our conversation was interpreted by Tsog's friend, Odon, the director of the Information and Education Centre in the same offices. The third member of our meeting was Kerstin, seconded from the German Development Agency, who was familiar with the concept of microcredit, and they all thought it might suit their clients. They have branches in all the *aimags* (provinces) and in over 100 villages, and Odon asked me for material to put in the newsletter. Funding will of course be a crucial factor, though once a pilot project has been completed, international funders may well be interested.

Mrs Nadmid said very little but addressed me with a grace and warmth that felt like a real connection, though apparently she spoke a Mongolian so poetic that Odon had some difficulty in translating. When I wrote to Odon on my return, I asked her to say to Mrs Nadmid that we had everything in common except a language. As I try to find a funder for them, I hope that our contact will continue.

CHAPTER 14
Resistance and Renewal

Faith is the sense of life, that sense by virtue of which man does not destroy himself, but continues to live on. It is the force whereby we live.

Tolstoy

A few hours into the journey from Ulaanbaatar to Siberia, I noticed that my fine Bolivian jacket, the jacket that I had carried through all the hot countries for use at this time, was missing. Stolen, presumably. Arriving in Siberia in March without a coat – great. This discovery was followed by a still more unnerving event. Another coat appeared – a tatty green anorak brought by a young woman who we at first thought wanted to push into our compartment, then dump her stuff there. We had already said no to a woman bearing blankets. Our young companions argued for some time in Mongolian but finally allowed her to leave the coat which she tucked very carefully behind theirs, hanging up beside the door. We naïvely thought that she too must be worried about having her coat stolen. But, later, as customs police spent hours searching the luggage of everyone except foreigners and finally led away a man and a number of women, including the blanket woman, it became apparent that we had unwittingly been party to contraband – possibly drug smuggling. The coat loomed large in our sight until we left the train.

It's not surprising that Russia doesn't get many tourists: they make it so hard to get a visa. We were told that it is in retaliation for the difficulties we put in the way of Russians wanting to come to Britain. The process was complicated by the fact that we had to get the visa on the hop. We had tried in Bangkok, but had run out of time. So, armed with our faxed invitation, plane ticket proving our exit date from Russia, but lacking the necessary coupon for the Trans-Siberian entry into Russia, which hadn't arrived from Beijing, we somewhat tremulously went to the Russian embassy in Delhi. We walked along the vast road full of embassies till we found the Russian one, explained we needed it quickly and to our amazement were told it would be ready next day. We danced with delight in the street, not believing our luck, till we noticed that we had been charged not $15, as we had heard him say, but $50. But, in Russia, we found that others had waited for days and paid double. We had been lucky.

The other reason foreigners do not flock to Russia is that as a country it gets a very bad press. Stephen had been convinced that it was a ghastly country, and he was resistant to our going there. No doubt the stories of the Mafia are true, and it is certainly the case that people can be rude and pushy, but in general my experience has been positive. To stand on Red Square or go round the Pushkin Gallery with hardly a tourist in sight is a privilege.

———

Siberia in the snow, how it ought to be. If independent, this would be the largest country in the world – some 14 million square kilometres. We had arrived at Listvyanka, a village on the shores of Lake Baikal, a lake of superlatives. It is the deepest, oldest lake in the world – some 20 million years old and 40 kilometres across to the mountains we could see on the other side. It is a living museum of flora and fauna, containing some two thousand recorded species, of which some 70% are to be found nowhere else in the world. An organism unique to the lake keeps the water pure, so, as it contains one-fifth of the world's fresh water, the lake is a huge source of drinking water. Its purity also means that one can see down about forty metres into its depths of 1,673 metres.

When we were there, this giant lake was completely frozen over. It was an awe-inspiring sight, with chunks of the palest aquamarine forced up at the edges, and the gentle sound of cracking as we walked past. The daytime temperature was currently around freezing point but the ice was some one-and-a-half metres thick, and safe to walk on till May, we were told, though I still felt nervous about doing it. We had arrived at the wrong time – too late for cross-country skiing, which we had set our hearts on, and too early for a hike and a picnic.

We stayed for three days with a family in a wooden house in the village, just yards from the lake. We had been met and were accompanied everywhere by our guide, Elya, who warmed up considerably when we arrived at the house – our hostess Rita, though the same age as her mother, was a close friend. The house was pretty, and had been made comfortable for the many tourists that stay there. In the sitting room that was off-limits for visitors, Rita's mother, Valentina, spent most of her time watching Brazilian soaps.

There was no bathroom. Like the Mongolians, the Siberians seem to wash seldom. The weekly sauna or *banya* in the outhouse was the main event, though the tap in the kitchen did have a curtain round it so more extensive washing was possible. There was no running water; what there was came from an electrified well. The lavatory was again a pit, but in a smart pine-clad outhouse with a green velvet seat cover as the entrance to the smelly void. Still not an inviting prospect for night visits.

Our first breakfast on arrival was an indication of things to come – and such a contrast to Mongolia. Huge quantities of wonderful home cooking: home-made jam, soups, *piroshki* (little pasties), *blinis* (pancakes). Ham and sausage and cheese at every meal. Sometimes caviar, sometimes *ormul*, the local fish from the lake. We were thoroughly spoilt. In fact I was sick after one over-rich meal – it was rather a shock to my digestion after what we had been used to.

As we sat at table with Rita, her partner, Sasha, Valentina and Elya, and talk flowed in Russian, I remembered more words and phrases, and wished I were staying longer. Discussions about politics and life in general revealed a sad attitude on the part of Rita and Elya. They felt that, although some things were better – the availability of food, and freedom to speak their mind – it would take another fifty years or so for things to improve properly. There are a few rich people, they said, but no middle class and many poor people. Elya, though a graduate and an English teacher, did not regard herself as middle class.

People cannot afford a car or to buy a home. We learnt to our surprise that Rita was a microbiologist; her partner Sasha a maths teacher; the driver a geologist. All make more money from jobs in the tourist trade than in exercising the professions they have been trained for.

Elya was an atheist, and only accompanied us to the lovely local church in Listvyanka out of duty. She and I went for a stroll along the shore of the frozen Lake Baikal one day, and she intimated that she had a problem, though she was coy about divulging its nature. It turned out to be about a former boyfriend, and the problem of being a strong woman. She was clever and pretty and felt, at 27, that life was passing her by. She wanted to get out of her small town, to Moscow, but felt she might have left it too late.

On the way back to Irkutsk to catch the train, Elya was back in severe guide mode. My parting with Valentina, on the other hand, was unexpectedly tearful. So emotional, we Russians! Valentina's two aunts emigrated to Canada and China respectively, and there was a lot of White support here during the Revolution. It all reminded me of my mother; I thought of her often while I was in Russia, and stopped the

Siberian silver birch

car to take a photo for her of silver birch trees – the image that haunts Russian exiles.

On the three-day leg of the train journey from Irkutsk to Moscow, our companions sharing the other two bunks of our compartment were a woman, her two teenage daughters, a cartload of luggage and a black cat. The mother (we never did catch her name though we had several friendly conversations) was a good looking and athletic woman, who dressed, bizarrely, in white frilly hot pants, with sheer tights underneath. As she vaulted up on to the top bunk Stephen wasn't sure where to look. When she went out into the corridor, the young men in the carriage stopped and stared, could not believe their luck. She too got off at every stop, to walk the cat on a lead on the icy platforms, her full-length leather coat flashing open to reveal her splendid legs. She gradually encroached into the next compartment, with first her luggage, and then one of her daughters taking up the top bunk. In that compartment were Liz and Andrew, a delightful pair of English musicians with whom we spent many hours chatting and playing cards – especially a vicious game called President which we had learnt in Listvyanka.

The hours slipped by pleasantly, actually five extra hours as we caught up with Moscow time. Not for nothing is this called the best train in Russia. Everything was spick and span, and our *provodnitsa*, Irina, her initial steely demeanour transformed into smiles and a mild flirtation with Stephen, came by every morning and painstakingly vacced the compartment. There were little tensions, of course – with our fellow travellers over the Muzak, between Stephen and me as to who faced forward. But I was able, at last, to read *War and Peace* – a perfect book for the journey, both in length and setting. Andrew in the next compartment was reading Dostoevsky.

And the landscape was enchanting: snow, firs, birch, frozen rivers and little wooden houses, each with its plot of ground and greenhouse with glass removed for the winter. How could anyone say this journey was boring? Stephen and I took turns to stand guard over our luggage as we left the train for these stops. On the whole, the stations were grey, tidy and characterless, with a few shops set back beyond some steps, little kiosks selling more or less identical items of chocolate, sweets and cigarettes, often a few independent sellers offering sausages or home-made dumplings. The air rang with the sound of clanging as the *provodnitsas*, smart in their identical long blue coats and grey fur hats, wielded their axes against the ice on the train's wheels.

On Easter Sunday I felt a pang as I thought of my children going to my mother's and eating the Russian Easter cake, *paskha*, which I make every year, and which I would not have this time, even though I was in Russia, since their Easter came long after we were gone. On day number four, we were finally on Moscow time, our body clocks awry – more awake than asleep at night. My mattress slithered to the floor at the least movement, the train temperature went up and down, and was mostly far too hot; the lavatories, which were locked in stations, always seemed to be locked at that moment in the middle of the night when the bladder was at bursting point.

We did not stay long in Moscow. As a Russian friend said: "Moscow is not Russia, it is a capital city," and we had friends to visit elsewhere. But we did stay with a Servas host and his family in one of those Soviet apartment blocks about which we had heard so much. Apart from us, there were four adults and two children in this two-bedroomed flat. All four adults were working, and still they were poor. This was a story we were to hear again and again, as employers do not – possibly are unable to – pay the wages. Our host, Mikhail, was a homeopath, his wife, Ina, a cosmetologist, his mother, Marietta, a teacher, and his father, Anatol, a technician as well as, at 63, a marathon runner who had competed all over the world, making the connections from which he helped to set up Servas Russia. They were hospitable but, disconcertingly, they did not eat with us. They flitted in and out and we never sat down with more than one of them at a time. We had the feeling that all was not well with the family, and that they were preoccupied. It was the first time that we had felt like paying guests (though we were not paying) and we did not like it. We offered to take the family out to eat, but in the end all we were able to contribute were some groceries and a cake.

The shops and cafés in Russia are still hard to find, often with little evidence of their existence on the street. Even when there is a sign, *"Produkti"* or *"Café"*, not being able to see beyond a firmly shut steel door makes one tentative about entering, and usually the service inside lives up to all the jokes. Food and other goods are now readily available, if you have the money, and queues have largely disappeared, but you can see how the queues formed, as in each small shop there are different counters for cheese, biscuits, sausage or light bulbs, forcing one to stand in line for each in turn.

There was a great deal of public drinking in Moscow. Many of the young people walked down the street, bottle of beer in hand – pushing a pram, hand in hand with a girlfriend, or a woman on her own, placing the empty bottle on the pavement. It was all horribly casual and habitual. But we were pleasantly struck by the Russian habit of simply flagging down a passing car in the street instead of calling a taxi. We did this with Russians and on our own, and in several towns found it a convenient way of getting about. Drivers are often keen to earn a bit of extra money if it does not take them too far out of their way. The destination and price is discussed, a deal is struck, and one is on one's way. It can't be such a dangerous country if climbing into a stranger's car is so common. We could not imagine doing it in Britain.

We went to Moscow Quaker Meeting, held in a suburb, on the stage of a community hall. It's a small but growing Meeting with some five members and a number of attenders. Several of them are well acquainted with other European Meetings, and one, indeed, is English, a woman who spends much of her time working with Chechen refugees in Ingushetiya. She and her colleagues do not now actually go into Chechnya since two volunteers, working partly under Quaker auspices, were kidnapped and held to ransom a year or so ago. Moscow Quakers are deeply involved in several projects in different parts of Russia. Under the auspices of Friends House Moscow, independent of Moscow Meeting, and in fact a British charity, they run Alternatives to Violence projects, and reconciliation, mediation and conflict prevention and resolution in many parts of the country. They conduct training in human rights, and give assistance to refugees and forced migrants, mainly from Chechnya. In many of these projects they are supported by British Quakers.

It was Stephen's first time in Moscow, and we did a little sightseeing – marvelling at the beauty of St Basil's, and of the world-famous icons in the Tretyakov Gallery. At the Pushkin Gallery, I was surprised to find, for the first time, that the Impressionists seemed strangely old-fashioned and "pretty". I found myself drawn to the drama and glorious colour of the Gauguins and Matisses: vivid reminders of the colours of our journey, in the South Seas, in India and in the Far East.

I first met Sasha and his mother Larissa about seven years ago, at Taizé, the ecumenical monastery in south-east France that attracts people from all over the world. I had not found Friends at that time, was still seeking to fill the need that had unexpectedly opened up in me. We became good friends, and Sasha and I have corresponded ever since.

The family lives in Kolumna, a town a couple of hours' train journey from Moscow. Expecting a dreary Soviet town, we found a pearl: churches of all shapes and colours, ancient city walls; a city founded in 1170, forty years after Moscow, but because of a military installation it was closed to foreigners until ten years ago. Larissa lives in a flat in an old wooden building, and Sasha and his wife, Inge, have a flat across the road, which, astonishingly, they handed over to us for the duration of our stay.

When Sasha came to us, I'm afraid he had to sleep on the floor. He had visited London a few years before, and we heard the terrible story of which his letters had given no indication – he didn't dare commit such things to paper. He had duly qualified as an English teacher, then was summoned by the KGB. They wanted him to work for them, and said that all his male classmates had agreed to do so. Sasha refused: it was against all his convictions and his strong Orthodox faith. They said that if he did not do so, they would ensure that he did not get a job. And so it proved. For many years Sasha was obliged to work unofficially, mostly as a window cleaner. He had married a Latvian woman, Inge, but at that time was only allowed to see her for three months in the year – the police would not sign the papers to allow him to live there or for her to become resident in Russia. He was desperate to move abroad – anywhere – but having signed a piece of paper when he came to England saying he would not try to stay, he honoured his commitment. Despite his poverty, he came with armsful of presents – chocolates, traditional Russian bark pictures and papier mâché lacquer bowls.

It was wonderful to see them again, and finally to meet Inge, a very bouncy, feminine and highly intelligent young woman with red cheeks, like a doll. Events had moved on. Although not officially resident in Russia, Inge now lives with Sasha, retaining her Latvian passport and a considerably freer situation than her husband, who finds it hard to get a visa to travel anywhere, though the whole family does manage to go to Taizé every year. Sasha had filled out and grown a moustache, Larissa was the same as ever though I had not recognised her when we bumped into her on the train.

We had heard from his letters that Sasha had managed to get a job, as a translator in a local factory; his mother had two jobs as a teacher and translator. Still they could not make ends meet – very few people in Russia get paid their whole salary; often only ten per cent. Anyone with a little land grows vegetables to keep body and soul together. Everyone in this country seems to grow, pick and pickle their own. Even Muscovites pick the wonderful mushrooms (*griby*) that we had in soup, and Larissa was growing peppers and aubergines on her window sill, and other vegetables outside. After my previous visit I had sent them seeds from England.

Despite their better circumstances, Sasha remained, perhaps not surprisingly, pessimistic about the future of Russia. "What can you expect with a president who used to be head of the KGB?" Pessimism is of course endemic in the Russian character, and reflected in their literature. The hopelessness that we encountered was pervasive. Elya in Siberia had felt it would take fifty years for Russia to "catch up" and was sure local elections were rigged, though she had some faith in national ones. Sasha had never voted, feeling that only a drop in voting figures would make an impact on an otherwise irredeemable situation. Only Mikhail had felt positive about the current administration.

But, unlike most that we met, Inge was able to make good use of her original psychology qualification by working as a Neuro-Linguistic Programming practitioner in Moscow three days a week, though she had to travel two and a half hours each way by bus. Larissa was due to get her pension in two years' time, at the age of 55, but she said she would not retire. No one, she said, stops work in Russia until they die. Her mother, who worked for 57 years, is living proof of that stress. At 78, she lies in her bed in Larissa's flat with a heart condition, afraid to move. Sasha is out of a job temporarily, and there is no unemployment benefit.

The flat was, it appeared, state-owned and thus rent-controlled at a level common throughout the country, depending only on the amount of space. In their case it was set at R200 a month. Larissa was living in the house her mother had been able to buy, ten years before, after *perestroika*. We heard awful tales of old people who are promised care on condition their carers inherit their property, then their "carers" leave them to die. Sasha said there had been an example in the flat below – horrible to contemplate as we watched neighbours come and go.

Also staying with the family were two builders and decorators from Uzbekistan, working locally and sending money home to their wives. In return for their accommodation the men sometimes did a bit of work for their hosts, but it was basically just as a kindness that they were allowed to stay. We only had one conversation with them – they kept themselves to themselves, and ate separately. Indeed, their cuisine was quite different from that in Russia.

The renaissance of religion in Russia has of course been underway for some time. Faith had not disappeared but just gone underground. When I had visited Moscow a few years before, it seemed that every church was being renovated: an enormous amount of time and money was flowing into the restoration of these lovely buildings. But on my previous visit too I had heard of how much money (estimated cost US $250 million) people were being expected to donate to rebuild the Cathedral of Christ the Saviour in Moscow, with domes again of pure gold. On this visit to Moscow I had unwittingly been taken to see the finished product – a repro-style monstrosity of very visible expense. The question of poor people giving to the church is as old as the church itself, however, and the principal point was the restoration of choice and freedom to worship, in which I delighted.

Our time in Kolumna was steeped in visits to local churches, glimpses of services in different buildings, congregations mainly of older women but with smatterings of men and younger people. Sometimes there was some singing, just a few lovely voices in harmony. On one walk round the town in a biting wind, in a borrowed coat, I went into a church in a monastery, and heard singing of tear-inducing beauty and precision – just two women's voices and one man's: perfect. Outside the glorious early evening sun and shadows greeted us.

I had been reading recently in Colin Thubron's *In Siberia* of Old Believers, a fascinating sect that had been hounded as heretics and, on hearing that there was an Old Believers' church in the town, we asked Sasha to take us. There was some doubt as to whether we would be allowed in – it is rather an exclusive sect – but in the event we were let in to stand at the back of the few worshippers in their headscarves and boots. Some of their beliefs are quite similar to those of Quakers, and the glimpse we had of their church showed it to be much simpler and barer than the usual ornate Orthodox churches with their wealth of gilded icons.

Inge, Larissa and Sasha at the bus stop

A deeper connection came from a visit to a fourteenth-century monastery, in process of restoration, some miles out of town. We were shown round by a joyous bearded young monk who expressed his assumptions about the divide between the cloistered and the worldly life. I expressed the belief that it is possible to obtain interior peace and joy while living in the world.

Because Sasha and his family are religious, we saw a Russia quite different from what atheist Elya had shown us. She said that, brought up as a Pioneer, she could only be an atheist, but Sasha, who had been forced to be a Pioneer, is deeply religious. We heard that he had been a rebellious Pioneer, and, foreshadowing his adult refusal to join the KGB, he had been the only child to have refused to go on to the next stage towards membership of the Communist Party. He told them: "I have been such a bad Pioneer, I think it would be harmful to the organisation if I were to join." Devout, pessimistic, but strong-minded, even at that age.

CHAPTER 15

Spring

The beauty of the world . . . is a relationship of the world to our sensibility . . .
The love of this beauty proceeds from God dwelling in our souls and goes out
to God present in the universe. It . . . is like a sacrament. Beauty is eternity
here below.

Simone Weil

We came home gradually. As we travelled confusedly through the five time zones of the Trans-Siberian Express, we were moving ever closer, to Europe and to England. Already in Siberia, on the shores of the deeply frozen Lake Baikal, we had noticed a difference in gesture, ways of talking that made us realise we were soon to be out of Asia. We didn't cross the boundary between Asia and Europe till a point in the Ural mountains some 3,500 kilometres further west, but we felt the intimations.

It was in St Petersburg, though, that we were forcibly hit by Europe and by spring.

St Petersburg, jewel of European civilisation, and my mother's birthplace. I had wanted to take her there for her eightieth birthday, but she would not go. Having left in 1920 with her mother and brother on the back of a hay cart, leaving her father for dead (he had in fact been imprisoned by the Bolsheviks and caught up with them later in Latvia), she had no wish to return.

"I was so glad to leave," she said, "I don't want to go back."

She had not been able to tell me where they had lived, except that it was close to the main street, the Nevsky Prospect. But she remembered riding on a horse-drawn sleigh as a small child, in the snow. A horse had stumbled and had been whipped. She had been upset: when she fell, she was cuddled.

I phoned her from St Petersburg, as I had from every country we had visited.

"Where are you?" she asked.

"I'm in St Petersburg."

Intake of breath. "Oh . . . and is it lovely?"

"Yes, Mum, it is lovely."

And so it was. Grand and gracious and beautifully proportioned. The long eighteenth-century buildings along the River Neva like a Canaletto painted in pastels. The Winter Palace in particular, a glory in pale green and gold; the ethnological museum turquoise and gold with a look of a wooden building – the first museum in the country. The Neva itself, flowing fast through the centre of the city, was thickened by little ice floes speeding downstream, reminders of a fierce winter just past.

Because we had hit spring. It was our first spring for two years (we had left before it had got underway in the UK) and we had forgotten how lovely it is. We had been travelling through extreme climates: the humid heat of the Southern States of the USA in August and Singapore; the severe cold of Mongolia; even the temperate heat of central India in winter. But nothing was like a European spring, with everything sparkling in the brilliant blue skies that we had been experiencing almost continuously since Beijing, but which now had a gentle warmth that melted the ice from the canals.

And I experienced Europe as if for the first time, and realised how much we take for granted. The richness of the culture; a city steeped in history – even if much of the history has been oppressive.

We arrived off the train in the early morning, with nowhere to stay. We had phoned a dozen or so Servas hosts the previous night from Moscow – phoning from Moscow had proved extremely difficult until we got to Leningradski station. But it was to no avail. The Servas list was out of date, and those hosts who were still at the same numbers were otherwise engaged. Before booking into a hotel, we tried just one more name: that of the co-ordinator of Servas, St Petersburg. Vladimir understood our predicament entirely. He explained in perfect English that he couldn't put us up, but at least we could leave our luggage. He had to go to work, but his daughter and father would let us in. He would see us in the evening and find someone to put us up.

And so it transpired. Vladimir actually popped back soon after our arrival to check that all was well – and we found a meeting of minds and spirit. He admired Quakers; he wanted us to meet his friends; at least we could all have supper tonight. And so, after a delightful harmonious though footsore walk round the town, Stephen and I shared the evening meal of soup and cottage cheese with him, his warm wife, Olga, their daughter, Lisa, a very articulate girl of 13, and Vladimir's father, who attended to his vodka as we talked. Of personality types – Olga's current preoccupation – of globalisation, of the real unity that binds people of different nationalities. This family too shared rooms: the father in one, and Olga, Lisa and Vladimir in the other. Not surprising that the parents did not get on too well. They were envious of our ability to travel even a day together, let alone a year. So perhaps we weren't doing so badly! Again they were two scientists who had given up their original callings. They seemed to enjoy their jobs, but it was such a waste. Vladimir asked if we would give a talk to Lisa's class at school. We were happy to agree.

What a man, what generosity of spirit and genuine interest in travellers and their needs. A true practitioner of international friendship, another whose service is in hospitality.

The first stay that he fixed up for us was in a children's art academy, a foundation which was trying to make a little money by letting out rooms, since they had no State support. It was a massive eighteenth-century building, in the process of being restored, but it was obviously a slow and expensive enterprise. We had a long thin bedroom on the third floor, up some very grand stairs, with a bathroom along an L-shaped corridor of dusty largely unused classrooms. We were the only people there apart from a woman on duty. There were no pupils, though I gathered a class was expected in the evening. We were able to wander around and look at the galleries of art but it all felt strangely empty and unfinished. We had agreed a price for our stay, but no one seemed to know to whom to pay it or what was due. I finally had to push money at them in what felt, despite my best Russian, like a sea of mutual incomprehension, and we swung the huge heavy door behind us.

Our next residence was chez Ekaterina, not a Servas host, but a friend of Vladimir's who generously allowed us to stay for several days in her large ramshackle apartment that used to house six families. She was a handsome woman in her forties who had travelled widely, principally in India, Tibet and China. She was influenced by Buddhism and tried to draw the best from all religions. Poor Ekaterina, who shared the flat with her daughter and a younger friend, Svetlana, was in a very difficult situation. One of her neighbours had knocked down a wall, actually appropriated part of her flat, and included it in her new enlarged kitchen. Ekaterina had called the police, been through all sorts of legal hoops, and got court orders that had not been implemented. It was probably another case of no bribe, no result. Having failed to get compensation, she was now struggling to get some paperwork to show her entitlement to the rest. But the owner of the building was now trying to sell and Ekaterina was frightened that she would not get all she was due. She was being bullied out of her flat, which with its generous proportions and high ceilings would evidently, once done up, be sumptuous. Ekaterina was a peaceful woman and simply did not want to spend any more of her depleted energies in contesting further.

Like other Russian hosts, Ekaterina would not eat with us, but served us excessive amounts in a flustered frenzy, saying, "It won't be long," and deprecating everything she produced. Having tried to help, we were reduced to sitting idly by. We did finally manage to take her and Vladimir out to a local café, The Idiot, to say thank you.

We were living just a block from the Maryinski theatre, home to the Kirov, and were able simply to walk round to book for the ballet. Here, at last, was the city culture Stephen had craved; a city to walk in, to breathe in, and to feel the balance of its eighteenth-century buildings and streets; the beauty of its baroque churches. And I was revelling in *War and Peace*, so many of its scenes set in these buildings, when czars held sway and the grand houses opened their doors to the gentry for parties and evenings of cards. In the blue and white glory that is St Nicholas, Stephen and I came upon a funeral service, with two bodies lying in open coffins; I only caught a glimpse of one serene face, then withdrew, not wanting to intrude.

As far as we could tell, there were only two Quakers in St Petersburg, and we had supper with one of them. Peter is an English composer, who had got a place at the St Petersburg conservatory six years ago, and had decided to make it his home: "a big fish", as he put it, "in a small pool". With a long bushy beard, he looked every inch the Russian intellectual, and had obviously established himself well: he had been a judge for various competitions, and had recently had a big premiere in Murmansk that was filmed by Swedish television. He had had great problems in getting a residency permit, and was not allowed to earn any money, so he taught a course in British contemporary culture free of charge. His service was, he felt, in sharing the everyday struggles of the Russian people. Half-Russian myself, I have always felt touched by that struggle that continues, unchanging, over the centuries. Under Czar or Bolsheviks, Stalinism or *perestroika*, the lot of the Russian people seems to be to endure.

From St Petersburg we flew to Stockholm, another fine European city on the water, and the scene of the last of those encounters with women that had been so rich for me throughout the year: Susan, Marion, Beth, Karol and now Margareta.

We had been bounced off our flight, and arrived in Stockholm four hours later than planned. I felt cheerful – perhaps the warmth of early spring in St Petersburg, perhaps the familiarity of Europe. I certainly had more energy, not having to struggle against adverse circumstances. Then we hit a blank wall at Stockholm station. Unable to get in touch with my singing teacher, who had said she might be able to put us up, no phone number for our Servas contact, too late to buy a phone card, we were saved by an English passer-by who spoke Swedish, and Directory Enquiries, and made contact with our Servas host.

After one night in Jerry's delightful artist's flat, up a little pine ladder to a charming attic and a mattress on the floor, we went to

Meeting with our luggage, and found that there was a room to be had in the Meeting House itself. Peace, no demands, self-catering, and the run of a splendid library 24 hours a day. The tranquillity that a building put to prayerful use has acquired over the past two hundred years. It was so good to be in a Quaker environment for our last three nights, to centre us again and prepare us for our return and all the adjustment it was going to call for. The only other residents were the warden, Margareta and her partner, Gerhard.

I felt that Margareta was where I wanted to be – in a life devoted to God – but she had been faced with much greater challenges. Having moved to Ireland many years ago, and married to an Irishman, she felt a strong pull to leave her husband and child and move back to Stockholm to introduce AVP to Sweden, which is what she was now doing. I cannot imagine such a terrible decision, but she said she felt called by God, that this was her mission. She had given up her house and all her possessions. This flat came with the job. When it was over, she had no idea what they would do, and she didn't mind. She had let go. She and Gerhard were the very day we met them in the process of giving away their car to someone who needed it more than they.

I don't like zoos, and it was somewhat by accident that I visited the one at Skaren, the first open air museum in the world. We watched the animals being fed, many of them not actually that keen – food comes too easily for wild animals in such circumstances. I found the sight of a large grey owl with a mouse hanging from its mouth repellent. I realised that I was developing what Quakers call a "Concern" about animals. Many years ago I wrote a piece for *Woman's Hour* against the keeping of pets, and that Sunday at Stockholm Meeting I ministered about our hypocrisy towards animals.

There are, of course, strong feelings about experimenting on animals and the wearing of fur in many countries, but our year of travels has heightened in me a wish to be close to the animal kingdom. The sightings we had of wild fauna on our journey were some of the most wondrous events – monkeys, alligators, otters playing, the dignity of elephants – and in New Zealand I saw for the first time how birds (and

I understand some animals in other parts of the world) behave when they are not afraid of human beings. What have we done to the animal world? Bred species only fit for our laps, or to be eaten – that could not now survive in the wild; shot them to stuff them and pretend they are alive; hunted them for fun – quite apart from the understandable killing for food. We rightly pay attention to factory farming but ignore the fish caught on a hook or, as we saw in Tonga, flailing on the decks of fishing boats, drowning in air. No one turns a hair.

It was cold in Stockholm. Spring deserted us until, on April 17th, 2002, a year to the day from our departure, we came home.

I had been dreading it, filling my emails with fears of a year's paperwork, the descent of responsibility. And typically, as I took the tube from Heathrow home, we were stuck for an hour and a half by a train breaking down in front of us outside Acton Town. Nowhere in the whole of our world travels did we endure such a delay – only for a

We appreciate very much presence with us of Jennifer and Steven and sharing with us their spiritual experience.

7.04.2002. Inno Polyurakhova, clerk of Mosco, Misde Roshchin, assistant Mell. of clerk.

14 April 2002
It was our joy to have Jennifer and Stephen with us this day – the last of their many stops with Friends around the world on this journey! They shared in our all-age worship with the theme of animals. Greeting to Westminster Friends!
Julia Ryberg, member of Clerks group, Sweden yearly Meeting

The last two endorsements on our Travelling Minute

demonstration in Bolivia or the rough waters of Lake Titicaca. What a reflection on London Transport!

But we were greeted by the most beautiful English spring, the loveliness of which I had forgotten: the greenness, the freshness of the trees, and the birdsong. I felt as if I were seeing England anew. Even London, which I had been so keen to leave, so sure that we would move from it on our return, was a pleasure. The multi-cultural richness that we had spoken of abroad, always with some secret negativity about the noise, dirt and overcrowded transport, seemed to be a real wealth, with a texture and variety that was wholly appealing. My flat, which I had always felt had its limitations and was a temporary measure, felt indeed like home. The blackbirds are still here in my little garden, and have been joined by a pair of robins and a pair of wrens; shopkeepers ask if I had a good time. Familiarity is very attractive. How easy it is!

Before we arrived, I felt a strong need to spend a few days alone in the flat, to sit, as it were, in the desert of my empty rooms, to adjust to being here. It was a spiritual need for space and contemplation that Stephen gracefully understood, and I think we both needed to think about things. We had agreed not to make any hasty decisions about continuing to live together, though much of what happened between us on the trip had been bruising. He agreed to spend a few days with his son and sister in Bristol while I found my feet here.

Of course it did not turn out like that. My daughter was the only one with a key, so I had to collect it from her, and at the same time, foolishly picked up my mail. After the first chilly night on my bare bed, wrapped in all my clothes, I had to collect some bedding from my mother's house, so arranged for all my belongings to come back – I did not in any case feel happy at burdening my mother any further, though I was not sure what I would do with all those books and clothes and ornaments. After a year living out of a rucksack I fully expected to want to shed a good deal of what I own. But, sadly, as soon as I opened the boxes I was delighted at the sight of things I'd forgotten I had.

May, 2002. A purpose-built room in a garden in Kent. I had gathered with a few other people, mostly strangers to me, for a seminar on one of the Upanishads. A couple of weeks earlier Stephen and I had attended a talk in London arranged by the Alister Hardy Association and given by Brother Martin from Santivanam. I had been invited to continue my interest in the subject for this more intense study session.

And it certainly was intense: quite hard coming to grips with the concepts underlying these mainstays of the Hindu scriptures, written over two thousand years ago. We began by reading an excerpt from Bede Griffiths' autobiography about a peak experience he had had as a child: an experience of the unity of nature. I had been reading a great deal of Bede Griffiths, and felt very close to this experience both through the reading and in my own path. We then read some moving accounts by "ordinary" people of their peak experiences before analysing the Kena Upanishad. Ken, our facilitator for the day, reads Sanskrit, and was able to interpret much of what we studied.

It was when we were discussing the breaking down of boundaries between the viewer and the viewed, the merging of sensibilities, that I felt an overpowering recognition. Ken said that when someone is asked to draw a tree, they usually begin by drawing their remembered concept of a tree, starting with the outline of a trunk, leaves and so on. But if they actually see clearly, feel one with the tree, they will indicate shade and colour quite differently, without boundaries. As he spoke of merging our sensibility with the tree, I felt such a merging quite powerfully. Drawn to the tree outside, I felt myself a part of it, at one. I at last understood why it is that I feel as I do in the desert: that my soul is expanding into the space, out to touch the horizon. I am part of that space, one with it.

This feeling of unity was so powerful that I was quite overcome. Knowing that tears were about to burst from me. I had to leave the room and lie down on the grass outside. I did indeed weep, sobbing with the intensity of the experience and with gratitude. I had to go round the world, and come back to England to have such an experience.

So, our travels were over. We were welcomed into the embrace of our families, friends and our Meeting. Much had happened and three members had died in our absence and, although we had been kept in touch by email, it took a while to settle back. It felt strange, especially, as two active Friends, not to be given any jobs to do, not be able to be of service to the Meeting. We were grateful to be given a breathing space, to let the effects of our trip sink into our deeper consciousness. We presented our Travelling Minute with its 27 endorsements to the Clerk of Monthly Meeting, and gave slide shows and talks at our own Meeting and at several others, sometimes together, sometimes separately – trying to share a little of what we had experienced.

The extract from George Fox that is quoted at the front of this book begins, *"Be patterns, be examples in all countries, places, islands, nations, wherever you come, that your carriage and life may preach among all sorts of people, and to them; then you will come to walk cheerfully over the world, answering that of God in every one."*

I like to think that we walked cheerfully over the world, and tried to answer that of God in everyone. Where we failed was in being patterns and examples. If God is love, and love is about relationships, then ours was not an example of unity. Stephen and I argued throughout, our egos and the strife between them often getting in the way of spiritual progress. We put on a brave face, indeed were harmonious, a good double act, when we were out on show: in our work and in our talks. It was in private that the problems arose. Shut in a single hotel room, we would bicker over the fan or the radio; with decisions to make every moment of the day, there were potential pitfalls every step of the way.

We often got to a point when separation seemed inevitable; indeed, it was often only practicalities, and the need to fulfil a commitment that kept us together. It is easy to blame the menopause, even easier to blame each other: the fact is, it was a real failure in a journey that otherwise taught us a great deal and changed us considerably.

In many relationships it is hard to get the right balance between independence and togetherness. For some individuals it seems there has to be a choice between a life of faith and one of emotional fulfilment. On our return to England I rang the Quaker solitary I had thought of in India. She told me a delightful story.

Much had happened to her since we had been in touch. She had had a particularly dangerous form of cancer but had survived the operation. She had then, in her sixties, received a phone call from a man to whom she had been engaged in her twenties. He had married someone else, and was recently widowed. He and my friend were now blissfully together.

"So, you're no longer a solitary," I said, somewhat ruefully.

She replied, "I was very happy then; I am very happier now!"

To the surprise of our closest friends, Stephen and I are still together, though the relationship has changed, inevitably. Sharing such a journey is a bonding experience and, with more space both literally and figuratively, we are less under pressure. I did not feel stressed while we were away, I felt stimulated; but there is no doubt that life at home is easier, and, even if I do not know what the future holds, staying put seems fine for the moment.

Before we left, I wrote that I hoped

To gain a new perspective, from seeing how life is in developing countries, away from the spoilt affluence of this insular part of the world; to learn to be less busy, to respond to the Spirit, to be more spontaneous; to be useful, humble, learning and contributing, to try to live in the present and respond to the needs that present themselves. It will change us – who knows how?

I certainly have changed. To quote Tom Dooley, I have "become more aware of myself and my soul's adventure", I have gained a new perspective, have become less busy and more spontaneous and have become a vegetarian. I am clear that I want to learn more from developing countries, to continue to listen to what other ways of life have to teach us. I have confirmed that for me faith is not just in "sacred" places but in the everyday, and heightened by encounters with people made extraordinary by their faith and by their lives, by our fellow creatures, and by the wild and elemental landscapes of the world.

The past year has been the next step in an internal journey, the end of which I do not know. It will take time for the experience to utterly fill my being. Then I will know what the next step might be. I am content, with Thomas Kelly, to be "walking with a smile into the dark".

Epilogue

The universe is a constant prayer
Vivekananda

The Spirit moves in mysterious ways, and in its own time. No obvious opportunity from our travels has drawn me back, but the pull of developing countries has led to an opening in Madagascar. And once I let go of my own frustrated attempts to explore the culture of Native Americans, an invitation arrived to set up a project in Pine Ridge Reservation in South Dakota, the poorest community in the western hemisphere. I paid an exploratory visit in autumn 2003, and hope to return.

Stephen and I did not stay together. The tensions during our year of travel took their toll, and Stephen never really settled back into my London flat. We remain close, however, bonded by our memories and by the continuing friendships with those we met on the way.

My pleasure at the rediscovery of my belongings faded quickly, and in July 2003 I gave much of my furniture to my children, sold my flat and embarked on a more peripatetic life, carrying with me little more than I had taken on our travels. I wish to live more lightly on the earth, able to move to where the work is, where the leadings draw me. Having lived a life of travel for a year, I now find that I do not want "a home", or know where I wish to be. This new phase is not about more travel, but another stage in letting go. Anthony Gormley spoke of "the profound experience of unknowing". I wish to embrace my unknowing, live a life in which geography does not matter, be, as Simone Weil wrote, "rooted in the absence of a place".

Another step on this unexpected and gift-strewn path.

Further reading

Quaker

Quaker Faith and Practice: the book of Christian discipline of the Yearly Meeting of the Religious Society of Friends (Quakers) in Britain. Britain Yearly Meeting, 1995

Advices and Queries. Britain Yearly Meeting, 1995

The Quaker Universalist Reader no 1. Landenburg, PA: Quaker Universalist Fellowship, 1986

Fager, Chuck, *Without Apology: a manifesto of liberal Quaker theology.* Bellafonte, PA: Kimo Press, 1996

Jones, Rufus M., *The Double Search.* Richmond, IN: Friends United Press, 1975

Jones, T. Canby, *Thomas Kelly as I Remember Him.* Wallingford, PA: Pendle Hill, 1988

Kelly, Thomas, *A Testament of Devotion.* Harper Collins, 1996 (first pubd 1941)

Woolman, John, ed. P. P. Moulton, *The Journals and Major Essays.* Richmond, IN: Friends United Press, 1989

Other faiths

'Abdu'l-Baha, trans. Shogi Effendi, *The Wisdom of the Master: the spiritual teachings of 'Abdu'l-Baha.* Ashland, OR: White Cloud, 2000

Chinmayananda, Swami, *We Must.* Sidhabari, HP, India: CTT Publications

———, *Solitude.* CTT Publications

———, *On the Path.* CTT Publications

Conze, Edward (selector and translator), *Buddhist Scriptures.* Penguin, 1971 (first pubd 1959)

Dyckman, K.M. and Carroll, P., *Inviting the Mystic, supporting the prophet: an introduction to spiritual direction.* Mahwah, NJ: Paulist Press, 1981

Gibran, Khalil, *The Prophet.* Oxford: Oneworld, 1998 (first pubd 1923)

Griffiths, Bede, *The Golden String.* Springfield, IL: Templegate, 1992

Happold, F.C. (ed), *Mysticism.* Penguin, 1991 (first pubd 1963); includes William Law and William Blake quotations

Huxley, Aldous, *The Perennial Philosophy.* Flamingo, 1994 (first pubd 1945)

Krishnamurti, J., *The Wholeness of Life.* Gollancz, 1978

Lawrence, Brother, *The Practice of the Presence of God.* Oxford: Oneworld, 1999

Lewis, C.S., *Letters to Malcolm: Mainly on Prayer.* Fount, 1998 (first pubd 1964)

Merton, Thomas, *New Seeds of Contemplation.* Burns & Oates, 1964

The Mother, *Notes on the Way.* Pondicherry: Sri Aurobindo Ashram, 1980

Nouwen, Henri, *Seeds of Hope.* Darton Longman & Todd, 1998

Pandit, M.P., *Spiritual Life*. Pondicherry: Dipti Publications, 1983

Rinpoche, Sogyal, *The Tibetan Book of Living and Dying*. Rider, revised ed. 2002

Roger of Taizé, Brother, *A Heart that Trusts*. Mowbray, 1986

Sinetar, Marsha, *Ordinary People as Monks and Mystics*. Mahwah, NJ: Paulist Press, 1986

Swahanander, Swami, *The Power of Prayer.* Sidhabari, HP, India: CTT Publications

Tagore, Rabindranath, *The Religion of Man*. Unwin, 1988

Traherne, Thomas, *Centuries of Meditations*. Mowbray, 1985

The Upanishads. Penguin, 1965 (new translation by Valerie Roebuck, 2003)

Vardey, Lucinda (ed.), *God in All Worlds: an anthology of contemporary spiritual writing*. Vintage, 1996

Vivekananda, Swami, *Is Vedanta the Future Religion?* Bourne End: Ramakrishna Vedanta Centre, 1982

Waddell, Helen, *The Desert Fathers*. Vintage, 1998 (first pubd 1936)

Watson, Elizabeth, *Guests of my Life*. Burnsville, NC: Celo Press,1979

Weil, Simone, trans. Emma Craufurd, *Waiting on God*. Fount, 1995 (first pubd 1951)

Travel

Bryson, Bill, *I'm a Stranger Here Myself.* Random House, 1999

———, *The Lost Continent*. Black Swan, 1999 (first pubd 1989)

Jensen, Jamie, *Road Trip USA*. Avalon Travel Publishing, latest edition 2002

Morris, Jan, *Among the Cities*. Viking, 1985

Naipaul, V.S., *India: a wounded civilization*. Picador, 2002 (first pubd 1977)

———, *India: a million mutinies now*. Heinemann, 1990

Thubron, Colin, *In Siberia*. Chatto & Windus, 1999

Microcredit

Yunus, Muhammad, *Banker to the Poor.* Aurum, 1998

Other non-fiction

Chaudhuri, Nirad C., *Autobiography of an Unknown Indian*. Hogarth, 1987 (first pubd 1951)

Dooley, Tom, *The Night they Burned the Mountain*. New York: Farrar, Straus & Cudahy, 1960

Galland, China, *The Bond Between Women: a journey to fierce compassion*. New York: Riverhead Books, 1998.

Gandhi, M.K., *Non-violence in Peace and War*. Ahmedabad: Navajivan Publishing House, 1962 (first pubd 1942)

————, ed. Thomas Merton, *Gandhi on non-violence*. New York: New Directions, 1965

García Márquez, Gabriel, trans. Edith Grossman, *News of a Kidnapping*. Cape, 1997

Russell, Bertrand, *The Conquest of Happiness*. Routledge, 1993 (first pubd 1930)

Seattl, Chief (based on, by Ted Perry). *No Quiet Place*, Pickpocket Books, 1993. For explanation of Ted Perry's authorship for *Home* (1971), a film about ecology, see www.snopes.com/quotes/seattle.htm

Tomalin, Nicholas & Hall, Ron, *The Strange Last Voyage of Donald Crowhurst*. Contemporary, 2003 (first pubd 1970)

Poetry and fiction

de Bernières, Louis, *Señor Vivo and the Coco Lord*. Vintage, 1992

Eliot, T.S., *Collected poems*. Faber & Faber, 1963

García Márquez, Gabriel, trans. Edith Grossman, *The General in his Labyrinth*. Cape, 1991

————, trans. Gregory Rabassa, *Collected Stories*. Penguin, 1994

Greene, Graham, *The Power and the Glory*. Vintage, 2001 (first pubd 1940)

Hemingway, Ernest, *To Have and to Have Not*. Arrow, 1994 (first pubd 1937)

Narayan, R.K., *A Tiger for Malgudi*. Penguin, 1984

Nordhoff, C.B. & Hall, J.N., *Mutiny on the Bounty*. Little, Brown, 1989 (first pubd 1932)

Spanish Short Stories, ed. Jean Franco. Penguin Parallel Texts, 1992

Steinbeck, John, *Cannery Row*. Penguin, 2000 (first pubd 1945)

Tolstoy, Leo, trans. A. & M. Maude, *War and Peace*. Penguin, 1997

Further information

Alternatives to Violence Project (AVP)

www.avpinternational.org

in UK The Old Painswick Inn, Gloucester Street, Stroud GL5 10G
telephone 0845 458 2692
www.avpbritain.org

Microcredit

The Grameen Bank
Mirpur 2, Dhaka 1216, Bangladesh
telephone 800 2 803 559
www.grameen-info.org

Results
www.results.org

in UK 25 Clemens Street, Leamington Spa, CV31 2DP
telephone 01926 435430
www.info@results-uk.org

Quakers

The Religious Society of Friends (Britain Yearly Meeting)
Friends House, 173 Euston Road, London NW1 2BJ
telephone 020 7663 1000
www.quaker.org.uk

Friends World Committee for Consultation
173 Euston Road, London NW1 2BJ
telephone 020 7663 1199
email: world@fwcc.quaker.org

Servas

www.servas.org

in UK The National Secretary, Servas Britain, 68 Cadley Road,
Collingbourne Ducis, Marlborough SN8 3EB
telephone 0208 444 7778
www.servasbritain.u-net.com

Women's International League for Peace and Freedom (WILPF)

1 rue de Varembe, Case Postale 28, 1211 Geneva 20, Switzerland
telephone 41 22 919 7080
www.wilpf.int.ch

in UK www.ukwilpf.gn.apc.org